WRITERS AND THEIR WORK

ISOBEL ARMSTRONG
General Editor

BRYAN LOUGH
Advisory Edi

William Hazlitt

WILLIAM HAZLITT

A self-portrait reproduced by courtesy of the Maidstone Museum and Art Gallery.

WW

William Hazlitt

J. B. Priestley R. L. Brett

Introduction by Michael Foot

Northcote House

in association with
The British Council

This edition, with new introduction and bibliography, first published in 1994 by Northcote House Publishers Ltd, Plymbridge House, Estover Road, Plymouth PL6 7PZ, United Kingdom. Tel: (0752) 735251. Fax: (0752) 695699.

British Library Cataloguing-in-Publication Data
A catalogue record for this book is available from the British Library

ISBN 0 7463 0745 4

Typeset by PDQ Typesetting, Stoke-on-Trent
Printed and bound in the United Kingdom by BPC Wheatons Ltd, Exeter

Contents

Introduction

Michael Foot

J. B. Priestley was an essay writer of the first order, a born essayist, or, more appositely in this context, a natural pupil of William Hazlitt. His own portrait of the master was, as readers can see here for themselves, not something dashed off in a moment, but the expression of a lifetime's experience; an example of the art worthy to take its place beside Hazlitt's best, in his own masterpiece, *The Spirit of the Age*. It is word perfect, almost thought perfect, and since that balance has been so skilfully struck, nothing written here must be allowed to disturb it. But in the past half-century, since Priestley wrote his British Council essay, or, more precisely, since he formed his firm judgement on these matters in the 1930s, several developments have still further enhanced the estimate of Hazlitt's greatness.

Not many decades ago, no such honour or pre-eminence would have been accorded him. Hazlitt was still regarded as an outsider: his politics or his morals or the two together still seemed to forbid his proper recognition. In the 1930s Priestley himself was regarded as hopelessly biased or mistaken when he mentioned William Hazlitt in the same breath as Charles Lamb. Priestley also wrote, then and thereafter, most perceptively and lovingly about Charles Lamb; indeed he probably understood better than anyone else the subtle, ever-changing appreciation of their competing virtues. Once, the palm was accorded without a contest to Lamb; but assuredly, now, Hazlitt has overtaken his friendly rival, and not even Priestley who did so much with such authority, first to resurrect Hazlitt and then to keep the scales weighing fairly, is here to witness the spectacle.

Priestley sometimes took the view that Hazlitt was more successful as an essayist than as a critic, but often no sharp distinction could be drawn between the two, and sometimes there were moments, famous or not so famous, when Hazlitt expressed the spirit of the age and put his own individual imprint upon it. Which was it when he heard his first recital of the *Lyrical Ballads* at Nether Stowey from the mouths of Wordsworth and Coleridge themselves, and 'the sense of a new style and a new spirit in poetry came over me'? (*The Complete Works*, vol. 17, p. 117). Which was it when he pronounced Wordsworth – and the Wordsworth of *The Excursions*, not *The Prelude* – the most original poet of the age? Which was it when he saw Edmund Kean perform as Shylock at the Drury Lane theatre on 26 January 1814, and when the whole future of the English theatre was so powerfully influenced, indeed more than that, for this was a political event? Relations between Jew and Gentile were to be transformed not merely here in Jew-baiting Britain but across the planet.

As it happens, not at all accidentally, three of the major new studies of Hazlitt which have appeared in recent years hinge on that scene, although of course they proceed later to deal with much else. David Bromwich describes, in his *Hazlitt: The Mind of a Critic*, published in 1984, how that encounter riveted his attention and opened for exploration regions of Hazlitt's mind which had never been explored before. Stanley Jones in his *Hazlitt: A Life, from Winterslow to Frith Street*, published in 1989, puts that bitter, glorious winter's night in its proper place in our literary history more surely than ever before. And Jonathan Bate in his *Shakespearean Constitutions*, published also in 1989, achieves the considerable feat, after so long an interval, of making a major addition to the stock of our Hazlittean–Shakespearean knowledge.

Altogether, the Edmund Kean affair was not just the consequence of some lucky accident. It was the achievement of Hazlitt's self-education in Shakespearean scholarship and Shakespearean understanding, a subject which Hazlitt himself had not sought to unravel directly for our benefit. It was curious that he should have become such a Shakespearean expert. He had soaked himself in several other writers long before – Fielding, Cervantes, Defoe, Swift, Rousseau, Burke, Montaigne. He longed to paint before he thought he could write, and took his ideas of composition into the theatre. He was for years much more interested in politics than literature. He saw the reality of the battles between right and wrong, between rich and poor.

But then, with a startling suddenness, he awoke to the

discovery that Shakespeare might be an ally in these contests, and once the late-developer realized what he had missed, he changed not merely his judgement about Shakespeare but his whole way of writing. Everything else he wrote thereafter became studded with Shakespearean arguments and allusions. Several of his particular verdicts changed the way the world thought about them, as the real force of his ideas overcame prejudice and ostracism. He was the first to insist that *Lear* was the greatest of the plays, the first to make Henry V step down from his flag-wagging pedestal; he rescued *Cymbeline* from near oblivion: all important triumphs on his part, if none could equal the transformation of Shylock.

But all these reassessments, all these variations in tone and accent, were they not political in origin? Were they not evidence rather of his constricted mind than of any soaring imagination? Whatever his merits as a critic, was it not a debasement to yield to politics such predominance? And was he not aware that Shakespeare, the politician, could normally be recruited as the defender of the established order and not solely by interested Tories like Dr Johnson but by a much wider company?

Hazlitt knew how to deal with these insinuations no less than the frontal attacks. He would take all such assaults head-on and hurl them back on his accusers. He expounded his full case in his treatment of *Coriolanus* and, even more expansively, whenever he got the chance, he presented on his stage a greater Shakespeare than his enemies had ever imagined – 'The capacious soul of Shakespeare', he wrote, 'had an intuitive and mighty sympathy with whatever could enter into the heart of man in all circumstances.'

And the mention of Dr Johnson's name should remind us how all-pervasive was his authority in matters of our literature and the language. To challenge him took some daring; but Hazlitt did it. He thought there was a better way of writing English, all the more urgently required since the common people wanted to join the political debate proceeding all around them. He had some good allies in those Revolutionary times, Thomas Paine and William Cobbett. Each wielded his pen in a new style; each wanted to join the revolt against Johnsonian suffocations. But Hazlitt was the one who understood best what he and they were doing. And they had another common master, along with Shakespeare. Each of them had been taught, from their childhood, by Jonathan Swift. Maybe that was just another reason why Dr Johnson would have liked to see the destruction of Swift, and why he almost succeeded. It was Hazlitt who led the counter-assault against the Johnsonian calumnies, and prepared the way for the revival in Swift's reputation both as a poet and a prose writer. He saw how *Gulliver's Travels* was 'an attempt to tear off the mask of imposture from the world; and nothing but imposture has a right to complain of it'.

Such was the manner in which Hazlitt could raise a literary argument to the highest level. He could do the same in so many fields: painters, philosophers, novelists, historians may return with the poets to learn from his original accomplishments.

Professor Brett was the first to note that Hazlitt was the first critic to take the novel seriously. Before that, Hazlitt had made himself an art critic – 'the best English critic before Ruskin', in the words of Lord Clark, and, of course, most famously, as we have seen, he had made himself a theatre critic. Though not a poet, he still made himself a critic of poetry to equal any other, even the poets themselves. And then his lecture 'On Poetry in General' still stands as one of the greatest in the language. Here, of course, he had many competitors, but none to beat him: Milton, Dryden, Pope, Coleridge, Wordsworth, Shelley, Byron, Keats, Arnold. When the full list is compiled, the feat becomes barely credible, and in one sense Professor Brett's discovery reveals the most remarkable of the lot. He read most of his novels in his youth and then, as constantly as he could, he would return to his favourites: Don Quixote, Moll Flanders, Gulliver, Tom Jones, Uncle Toby, the great discoveries of modern, even 'modernist' times. Swift and Sterne were both folded to Hazlitt's bosom. Hazlitt believed that the imaginative powers of his novelists were to be respected as much as the poets' – especially since they often showed themselves more constant in their politics.

Yet, with so much accomplished and so much still to come, he came near to casting it all away in one brazen emotional spasm of ineptitude and humiliation. Or so it seemed to his enemies and his friends at the time and for a long while thereafter. His love affair with Sarah Walker and what he himself made of it in his *Liber Amoris* has become a major issue in the debate about his whole life and achievement – as he himself may also have intended.

Priestley himself touches on the matter without any effort to probe deeply when he describes how Hazlitt 'was crazily infatuated (a fine example of *anima* projection, Jungians please note) for almost half his forties with his landlady's daughter, Sarah Walker, a sly minx'. And before Priestley, quite a number of passionate admirers of Hazlitt, headed by Robert Louis Stevenson, have been put off writing his life or put off Hazlitt altogether by this single little volume, *Liber Amoris*. Priestley was not being prudish or censorious in any sense whatever, and his Jungian diagnosis was clearly intended to offer an intelligent clue to the whole business.

But we have all become somewhat less constrained in these matters of delicacy since then. Priestley wrote his essay in 1960, but in 1970, Penguin Selected Writings, edited by Ronald Blythe, printed the *Liber Amoris* in full in the proper place, alongside his other writings. It was not precisely thus that Hazlitt himself would have had the piece appear; he must have known what risks he ran, how his Tory enemies would pounce, how his great political causes might thereby be injured. So ferocious was the hostility provoked by *Liber Amoris* that he had to take his name off his next volume of essays – as it happened the collection of his masterpieces, *The Spirit of the Age*. He was made to suffer almost unendurably, and the wound must have cut all the deeper because he knew he had brought it upon himself. Yet he had to write it; he could not suppress it; it was the truth.

It may also be that the author who saw so much of his own passionate nature distilled in these pages still thought it to be a work of art. Whatever the sensitiveness of others, he had no compunction in reading or writing such confessions. Indeed, the favourite book of his youth, almost without compare, although the competition was severe, was Rousseau's *La Nouvelle Héloïse*. How much poorer both he and the world would have been if that contrived confession, more moving still than the real *Confessions* which came later, had never been published. How much both the precedents and the prevailing Romantic atmosphere might be responsible for Hazlitt's action was discussed by Marilyn Butler in a paper published in 1984 with the provocative title: 'The Long Tradition of Hazlitt's *Liber Amoris*'. It was at least indisputable that, despite all the contrary suggestions, which inferred that Hazlitt was driven to write solely by some blind, uncontrollable impulse, there was much deliberation in the work. Moreover, he continued reading and writing on several other themes – he had to do so, since he earned his livelihood that way. He could still examine his own motives and ambitions and dreams with the same objectivity as he had always had. He happened to be reading Byron's latest tragedy *Sardanapalus* at the very hour when he was reaching the height of the affair, and he saw the likeness between Sardanapalus's Myrrha and his own Sarah. 'Myrrha is most like S.W., only I am not like Sardanapalus', he wrote, and Sarah at least, if she had known, should have been gratified:

> So shalt thou find me, ever at thy side
> Here and hereafter, if the last may be.

The present writer once had in his hands the little exercise book – 'a small unbound octavo volume', according to the catalogue – in which Hazlitt started to write his love story, in his usual unfaltering hand – 'begun at Stamford on 29 January 1821'. It was genuine for sure, and was on sale at Sotheby's next day, 22 July 1985, after having been lost for years. It could not be cited as evidence finally to prove or disprove the Marilyn Butler theory. But one strand in her argument was incontestable: Hazlitt wanted the world to know what was in his heart. But that was still only one part of the story.

Soon after Priestley's book on Hazlitt was published, the present writer again received a letter from him. 'Before you do the Sarah Walker episode in your Hazlitt life you should have an hour's talk with me, because this is the best example I know of Jung's "projection of the anima", and it should be discussed in these terms.' Indeed it should, but we did not have the chance to return to the topic. However, it always seemed to me that an earlier psychoanalyst, who knew Hazlitt even better than Priestley, had prepared the way.

Before Priestley, but still well over a hundred years after Sarah – that 'sweet apparition', or, if you wish, that 'slimy, marble varnished fiend' – had turned her glance so fatally upon Hazlitt, Charles Morgan wrote in the year 1948 an entirely new kind of introduction to the despised volume, in which he invoked the case knowledge of modern psychology, partly to explain Hazlitt but, even more remarkably, to reveal how much of modern discoveries in this field Hazlitt had anticipated. Morgan also made a most discriminating comparison between Hazlitt and Stendhal, Hazlitt's contemporary whom he resembled in so many aspects, although most notably not in philandering bravado or technique. Just at the moment when Hazlitt was making obeisance before the statue he had erected, Stendhal was writing his own book of love, *De l'Amour*, in which the Hazlittean trauma, disease, madness, idyll, is immortally diagnosed.

Soon afterwards the two men met in Paris. Stendhal gave his book to Hazlitt who must have read it on his journey onwards towards the two mistresses they shared, Rome and Venice. How Hazlitt's hair must have stood on end as he turned over those burning pages; how he must have marvelled at this French sympathizer who understood his predicament with Sarah so much better than his own countrymen (and how he must have concealed the volume from his new sedate wife who was making part of the journey with him).

'She is dead to me, but what she once was to me can never die.' That was Hazlitt's own epitaph on the affair, but perhaps Stendhal even helped finally to soothe his passion. And as Morgan shows, there was one sense in which he carried the investigation further even than Stendhal or Montaigne, two acknowledged mentors; he 'shows' – in the words of Morgan – 'because he is a supreme realist and is unafraid to give himself away, that the crystallising lover is by no means the blind fool that he is traditionally supposed to be. He thus deprives himself of the only romantic defence with which an aloof and self-righteous world might be disposed contemptuously to cover him. The lover, Hazlitt says in effect, is not even a dupe; he is worse, he is a half-dupe, and yet persists'. Hazlitt made himself, again in Morgan's memorable conclusion, 'the sane, unsparing analyst of his own madness'. And yet Stendhal conducted the analysis afresh, and with an even greater clinical precision, and with a sense of humour too (and even with an invocation of the name of Montaigne, sacred to Hazlitt certainly), to recall sexual fiascos as remarkable as his own. Hazlitt surely must have been gratified to be assured, after such painful torture and on such high combined authority, that he was not so abnormal a creature after all.

As for Hazlitt's sanity, so often and interestedly questioned by his political enemies, his friends may take pleasure from the fact that plumb in the middle of the months when he obsessively and vainly waited for a soft word from Sarah, he could still sit down and write a five-thousand-word letter to his ten-year-old son (suitable for later publication, to be sure), one of the most civilized documents ever written by any father to any son:

> It is a good rule to hope for the best ... Never anticipate evils ... Learn never to conceive prejudice against others, because you know nothing of them ... Never despise anyone for anything he cannot help – least of all for his poverty ... Never despise anyone at all ... True equality is the only true morality or true wisdom ... Believe all the good you can of everyone ... Envy no one, and you need envy no one ... Never quarrel with tried friends or those who you wish to continue such ... Be neither a martyr, nor sycophant ... Do not gratify the enemies of liberty by putting yourself at their mercy ...

If Hazlitt had been distracted from his proper political duties, that last sentence to his son showed that he had some inkling of it himself.

Stendhal, 'My friend, Mr Beyle', did help to cure Hazlitt – not perhaps that he wanted to be just cured; what Sarah had meant to him, he insisted, would never die. It was necessary that somebody should approach this aspect of the subject with the relish and understanding of a Stendhal. Hazlitt and Stendhal were kindred spirits even if their methods of love making may have been very different: the one after all had been reared amid the severities of Celtic nonconformity while the other was testing the novelties of Milan or Venice. The writings of both on these tender themes are as essential for the proper appreciation of those times as their devotion to the ideals of the French Revolution. The best way to understand Hazlitt is to read Stendhal and vice versa. Each had some inkling of the genius of the other – long before other observers had interpreted the first signs. Each felt in their own experience the conquests and the defects of the Revolution and the Napoleonic Age. Late in the 1980s – in 1989, to be precise, which was a proper moment to initiate those Revolutionary celebrations – Stanley Jones's new life of Hazlitt was produced, which wove together the common English and French inspiration.

Indeed, Hazlitt did recover to write in that last decade some of his greatest essays. He had in himself something of the capacious soul he saw in Shakespeare; at least this association was why Shakespeare came to displace all his other heroes. As Hazlitt describes his Shakespeare, he unconsciously delineates some of his own features, not in any pretentious manner but as part of his growing discernment. Tragedy, he said, 'gives us a high and permanent interest, beyond ourselves, in humanity as such. It makes man a partaker with his kind. It saddens and softens the stubbornness of his will. It opens the chambers of the human heart. It is the refiner of the species: a discipline of humanity.'

Precious few of Hazlitt's great contemporaries foresaw the place which he was to occupy in our literature. Most of them – Wordsworth, Coleridge, Southey, Byron, and Shelley – were so outraged by the particular judgements he passed on them that they would not pause to see what it was he was truly saying and how he was saying it so well that his criticisms would live when theirs were forgotten. He was raising the essay to a new level as an art, he was discovering a new manner to express the spirit of the age, a new means to ensure that words were things, the faculty of writing which he admired most in his idol, Edmund Burke, but which he wanted to enlist in the cause of the Revolution. He had had that dream before he had the capacity to put pen to paper, and then, against all the odds, he carried it into effect.

Almost the only one among his contemporaries who did recognize his qualities was John Keats; part of his own inspiration came from hearing Hazlitt and reading him. He attended the same lectures with the young engraver, William Bewick, who offered the most memorable description of Hazlitt: 'the Shakespeare prose writer of our glorious century; he outdoes all in truth, style and originality'. Keats and Bewick saw the same man; his features became indelible. And yet the date of that meeting was 1819, before the appearance of what a later age would reckon as at least half the greatest of Hazlitt's essays.

He had a poet's insight into the world and a poet's imagination with not a trace of the egotism, sublime or otherwise, which Keats could sometimes associate with that calling. 'The suffrage of posterity' was Hazlitt's own phrase, and he could not fail to be gratified to see how it enabled his own ideas to survive and prosper – even the outrageous *Liber Amoris*.

William Hazlitt

J. B. Priestley   R. L. Brett

The Supreme Essayist

J. B. Priestley

I

'They are never less alone', wrote Hazlitt of authors, 'than when alone. Mount them on a dinner-table, and they have nothing to say; shut them up in a room by themselves, and they are inspired. They are "made fierce with dark keeping". In revenge for being tongue-tied, a torrent of words flows from their pens, and the storm which was so long collecting comes down apace. It never rains but it pours. Is not this strange, unaccountable? Not at all so ... Till they can do justice to the feeling they have, they can do nothing ... What they would say (if they could) does not lie at the orifices of the mouth, ready for delivery, but is wrapped in the folds of the heart and registered in the chambers of the brain. In the sacred cause of truth that stirs them, they would put their whole strength, their whole being into requisition; and as it implies a greater effort to drag their words and ideas from their lurking-places, so there is no end when they are once set in motion. The whole of a man's thoughts and feelings cannot lie on the surface, made up for use; but the whole must be a greater quantity, a mightier power, if they could be got at, layer under layer, and brought into play by the levers of imagination and reflection. Such a person then sees farther and feels deeper than most others. He plucks up an argument by the roots, he tears out the very heart of his subject. He has more pride in conquering the difficulties of a question, than vanity in courting the favour of an audience. He wishes to satisfy himself before he pretends to enlighten the public ...'[1]

Who reads Hazlitt now? The casual manner and flattened style of our younger writers do not suggest his influence. His is not one of the voices their own unconsciously echo. Perhaps Hazlitt is out,

[1] 'On the Difference Between Writing and Speaking'.

even among the captive readers of 'Eng. Lit.' No matter: if reading is to continue, he will come back. When I was first beginning to write, over forty years ago, I read him at all hours; he was then my favourite, my model author, and the only one who directly influenced my own writing. To explain and to praise him here is merely to make a first payment reducing the old debt. Except for professors and students, reading is not a compulsory activity; nobody outside the trade should be expected to enjoy every author of genius; many readers of these pages may have decided long ago that Hazlitt was not to their taste; but there must be some, especially among the young, who will relish, admire, perhaps love, this author when they come to make his acquaintance, and it is chiefly to them that I now address myself.

II

Hazlitt is usually described as an essayist and a critic. I would prefer to call him an essayist and leave it at that. He was a very fine critic of literature and the drama and acting, but he was not a diligent and systematic critic, devoting his life to the appraisal of other men's work; most of his criticism is to be found in hastily composed lectures. His main subject was not other men's work but himself, and for this reason he is best considered as an essayist. He preferred above anything else to tell us what William Hazlitt thought and felt about everything, and it is doubtful if anybody else in our literature succeeded better in this self-imposed task. After we have read him, we know Hazlitt as we know few other authors: it is as if we had sat up late with him night after night. Most of his pieces are scattered parts of some gigantic unplanned autobiography. And all this – for my money, as the Americans say – makes him an essayist.

How good an essayist? As usual, estimates differ. Thus Virginia Woolf, reluctantly compelled to admire him though not to like him (few women did: it was his chief misfortune), tells us that his essays cannot be included among the best; they lack unity, a mind in harmony with itself; Hazlitt was too much a divided man, lacking the integrated nature of the supreme essayists, their reticence, their composure. Now this is true enough, but I for one disagree sharply with the conclusion she draws from it, if only because the qualities she finds missing in Hazlitt do not seem to me essential for the best work in this form. In place of unity, harmony, reticence, composure, Hazlitt offers us variety, frankness, intensity, richness, the result of the division in his mind, the tension between the opposites, the lack of that integration always difficult for a large, broadly based, richly experiencing nature.

It is the difference between a neat packet of sandwiches and an untidily packed but splendidly luscious luncheon basket. You risk both indigestion and satiety but eat joyously and are well nourished. The very weaknesses that made Hazlitt difficult as a man, bringing disaster and anguish, are his strength as an essayist. So to many of us, not unacquainted with this form of writing, not only does he not fall short of the best, he is in fact himself the very best. If I were compelled to restrict my reading to one man's essays, that man would be William Hazlitt.

Among famous last words are the dying Hazlitt's 'Well, I have had a happy life'. His own life was hard, his death early, but there is much in the essays to explain that remark, which has seemed to many strangely pathetic and demonstrably untrue. 'The love of life', he wrote, 'is, in general, the effect not of our enjoyment, but of our passions. We are not attached to it so much for its own sake, or as it is connected with happiness, as because it is necessary to action. Without life there can be no action – no objects of pursuit – no restless desires – no tormenting passions. Hence it is that we fondly cling to it – that we dread its termination, as the close, not of enjoyment, but of hope. The proof that our attachment to life is not absolutely owing to the immediate satisfaction we find in it is that those persons are commonly found most loath to part with it who have the least enjoyment of it, and who have the greatest difficulties to struggle with, as losing gamesters are the most desperate.' In the same essay he pointed out that: 'the vehemence of our passions is irritated, not less by disappointment than by the prospect of success',[1] and of the active side of his life this was certainly true. On the passive side, in solitude, 'living to himself' as he called it, he found the enjoyments which in more superficial men the agonies of his active life might have been sufficient to quell completely. Not so with Hazlitt. 'What I mean by living to one's-self is living in the world, as in it, not of it: it is as if no one knew there was such a person, and you wished no one to know it:

[1] 'On the Love of Life'.

it is to be a silent spectator of the mighty scene of things, not an object of attention or curiosity in it; to take a thoughtful, anxious interest in what is passing in the world, but not to feel the slightest inclination to make or meddle with it. It is such a life as a pure spirit might be supposed to lead, and such an interest as it might take in the affairs of men: calm, contemplative, passive, distant, touched with pity for their sorrows, smiling at their follies without bitterness, sharing their affections, but not troubled by their passions, not seeking their notice, nor once dreamt of by them. He who lives wisely to himself and to his own heart looks at the busy world through the loopholes of retreat, and does not want to mingle in the fray... He reads the clouds, he looks at the stars, he watches the return of the seasons, the falling leaves of autumn, the perfumed breath of spring, starts with delight at the note of a thrush in a copse near him, sits by the fire, listens to the moaning of the wind, pores upon a book, or discourses the freezing hours away, or melts down hours to minutes in pleasing thought.[1]

Much of his time was thus spent in private, and it was such happiness that he doubtless recalled on his deathbed in 1830, in Frith Street, Soho. He was then only fifty-two, prematurely aged and suffering from cancer of the stomach; he was penniless; his one child still living, a son, did not return his affection; both his marriages had been failures, absurd failures too, and the one great love affair of his life, which had almost made a maniac out of him, had slipped from tragedy into squalid farce; he had for years been abused, libelled and slandered without mercy; he had long lived from hand to mouth, usually in great discomfort, writing hurriedly to keep his creditors at bay, quarrelling with his friends and multiplying his enemies, all in a narrowing world that denounced and rejected the revolutionary ideas that inspired him in youth and never afterwards left him; yet he meant what he said – he always did – when he declared with his last breath that he had had a happy life.

III

He was born in 1778, the youngest son of a rather feckless Unitarian minister, to whom Hazlitt never ceased to acknowledge his debt. 'After being tossed about from congregation to

[1] 'On Living to One's-Self'.

congregation in the heats of the Unitarian controversy, and squabbles about the American war, he had been relegated to an obscure village, where he was to spend the last thirty years of his life far from the only converse that he loved, the talk about disputed texts of Scripture and the cause of civil and religious liberty . . . My father's life was comparatively a dream; but it was a dream of infinity and eternity, of death, the resurrection, and a judgement to come.' And again, rather sadly: 'My father was one of those who mistook his talent after all. He used to be very much dissatisfied that I preferred his Letters to his Sermons. The last were forced and dry; the first came naturally from him. For ease, half-plays on words, and a supine, monkish, indolent pleasantry, I have never seen them equalled.' Bearing in mind that Hazlitt, somewhat to his father's disappointment, never entered the priesthood, a good deal of what he said about his father may equally well be applied to himself. With his father particularly in mind, he wrote of Dissenting ministers: 'We have known some such, in happier days . . . Their youthful hopes and vanity had been mortified in them, even in their boyish days, by the neglect and supercilious regards of the world; and they turned to look into their own minds for something else to build their hopes and confidence upon. They were true Priests. They set up an image in their own minds, it was truth: they worshipped an idol there, it was justice. They looked on man as their brother, and only bowed the knee to the Highest.'[1]

In pursuit of happiness Hazlitt senior left England for Ireland, Ireland for America, where he was never in one place long, then finally returned to England, settling at Wem in Shropshire. Thus William was a much-travelled child by the age of ten; and now he began to open out into adolescence. 'When the strong spell of childhood had just been broken, and even as I cast my eyes longingly upon the blue tops of the lofty hills in the distance and realised that there was a world beyond the blissful world of my immediate experiencing I began to realise that there was a world of thought and feeling too as to which I could only conjecture dimly, and to which I could in some measure find my way through reading – I can see myself with a book in my hand, seated outside in the sun even on cold days with a sheltering wall at my

[1] 'My First Acquaintance with Poets. On Court Influence'.

back, perhaps flushing slightly as the thought awoke in me that one day I might too write a book; perhaps seeing not the actual letters, but the letters that compose the word Fame glittering on the page before me.'

To these innocent years of growing awareness Hazlitt always looked back from his later unhappiness. Writing of himself as a boy, he said: 'He has only to feel, in order to be happy; pain turns smiling from him, and sorrow is only a softer kind of pleasure ... See him there, the urchin, seated in the sun, with a book in his hand, and the wall at his back. He has a thicker wall before him – the wall that parts him from the future. He sees not the archers taking aim at his peace; he knows not the hands that are to mangle his bosom. He stirs not, he still pores upon his book, and, as he reads, a slight hectic flush passes over his cheek, for he sees the letters that compose the word FAME glitter on the page, and his eyes swim, and he thinks that he will one day write a book, and have his name repeated by thousands of readers, and assume a certain signature ... Come hither, thou poor little fellow, and let us change places with thee if you wilt; here, take the pen and finish this article, and sign what name you please to it; so that we may but change our dress for yours, and sit shivering in the sun, and con over our little task, and feed poor, and lie hard, and be contented and happy, and think what a fine thing it is to be an author, and dream of immortality, and sleep o'nights.'[1]

In 1793 Hazlitt went to the New College, Hackney, an establishment for the sons of Dissenters; and while there he discovered the theatre and acting of Mrs Siddons, about whom he later wrote: 'The total impression (unquestioned, unrefined upon) overwhelmed and drowned me in a flood of tears. I was stunned and torpid after seeing her in any of her great parts. I was uneasy, and hardly myself, but I felt (more than ever) that human life was something very far from being indifferent, and I seemed to have got a key to unlock the springs of joy and sorrow in the human heart.' And again: 'To the retired and lonely student, through long years of solitude, her face has shone as if an eye had appeared from heaven.'[2] 1793 was also the year His Majesty's Government declared war on France, giving young Hazlitt a shock from which he never really recovered. As he wrote many years later: 'It seems

[1] 'The Dulwich Gallery'.

[2] 'On Novelty and Familiarity. A View of the English Stage'.

to me as if I had set out in life with the French Revolution, and as if all that had happened before that were but a dream. Certainly there came to me at that time an extraordinary acceleration of the pulse of being. Youth then was doubly Youth. It was the dawn of a new era; a new impulse had been given to men's minds, and the sun of Liberty rose upon the sun of life in the same day, and both were proud to run their race together. Little did I dream in those two years, while my first hopes and wishes went hand in hand with the human race, that before long the dawn would be overcast and set once more in the night of despotism ...'[1] So the enemies of the Revolution seemed to him, for the rest of his life, the enemies of the wonder and glory of his childhood and youth, the haters of happiness, so many life-destroyers.

He was so passionate about his political opinions because in fact they were more than political opinions. Even more of his heart than his mind was in them. Though capable of writing about politicians with notable acuteness, Hazlitt was not strictly a political thinker. So he felt that to reject the Revolution, as Wordsworth and Coleridge finally did, was to reject for ever the hope, wonder and glory of youth. And how he scolded them! In a study of Coleridge in *The Spirit of the Age*, twenty years after the poet's defection, he wrote: 'He has nerved his heart and filled his eyes with tears, as he hailed the rising orb of liberty, since quenched in darkness and in blood, and has kindled his affections at the blaze of the French Revolution, and sang for joy, when the towers of the Bastille and the proud places of the insolent and the oppressor fell, and would have floated his bark, freighted with fondest fancies, across the Atlantic wave with Southey and others to seek for peace and freedom – "In Philarmonia's undivided dale!" Alas! "Frailty, thy name is *Genius*!" What is become of all this mighty heap of hope, of thought, of learning and humanity? It has ended in swallowing doses of oblivion and in writing paragraphs in the *Courier*. Such and so little is the mind of man!'

Because Napoleon flashed like a thunderbolt out of the Revolution ('It awaited his appearance to triumph and to perish with him'), then he could do no wrong; so that Hazlitt's last weary years, when he was still capable of writing essays that were masterpieces, were mainly devoted to producing a huge life of

[1] 'On the Feeling of Immortality in Youth'.

Napoleon, a gigantic folly that sprang from his strong continuing belief in revolutionary principles. 'Let all the wrongs', he cries: 'Let all the wrongs public and private produced in France by arbitrary power and exclusive privileges for a thousand years be collected in a volume, and let this volume be read by all who have hearts to feel or capacity to understand, and the strong, stifling sense of oppression and kindling burst of indignation that would follow will be that impulse of public opinion that led to the French Revolution. Let all the victims that have perished under the mild, paternal sway of the ancient *régime,* in dungeons, and in agony, without a trial, without an accusation, without witness, be assembled together, and their chains struck off, and the shout of jubilee and exultation they would make, or that nature would make at the sight, will be the shout that was heard when the Bastille fell! The dead pause that ensued among the Gods of the earth, the rankling malice, the panic-fear, when they saw law and justice raised to an equality with their sovereign will, and mankind no longer doomed to be their sport, was that of fiends robbed of their prey: their struggles, their arts, their unyielding perseverance, and their final triumph was that of fiends when it is restored to them!'[1]

Having decided against entering the Unitarian ministry, Hazlitt passed his later teens and early twenties learning to paint and then doing some portraits for a living, but also wondering if he ought not to devote himself to metaphysics, a surprising alternative: as if a man could not decide whether to be Rubens or Spinoza. Here is Virginia Woolf's divided man, split between pure ideas and a deeply sensuous feeling for the world, with unity and harmony never to be achieved; but in a place somewhere between these two extremes, a place of summer storms and lightning flashes produced by the tension between them, Hazlitt's best work, his unique contributions to the Essay, were done.

But he took time. He spent years, mostly working or walking in solitude, finding himself. 'For many years of my life', he wrote, 'I did nothing but think. I had nothing else to do but solve some knotty point, or dip in some abstruse author, or look at the sky, or wander by the pebbled sea-side –

> To see the children sporting on the shore,
> And hear the mighty waters rolling evermore

[1] 'The French Revolution', in *The Life of Napoleon.*

I cared for nothing, I wanted nothing. I took my time to consider whatever occurred to me, and was in no hurry to give a sophistical answer to a question – there was no printer's devil waiting for me. I used to write a page or two perhaps in half a year; and remember laughing heartily at the celebrated experimentalist Nicholson, who told me that in twenty years he had written as much as would make three hundred octavo volumes. If I was not a great author, I could read with ever fresh delight, "never ending, still beginning", and had no occasion to write a criticism when I had done. If I could not paint like Claude, I could admire "the witchery of the soft blue sky" as I walked out, and was satisfied with the pleasure it gave me. If I was dull, it gave me little concern; if I was lively, I indulged my spirits. I wished well to the world, and believed as favourably of it as I could. I was like a stranger in a foreign land, at which I looked with wonder, curiosity and delight, without expecting to be an object of attention in return. I had no relations to the state, no duty to perform, no ties to bind me to others: I had neither friend nor mistress, wife nor child. I lived in a world of contemplation and not of action.'

Hazlitt then goes on to describe the ill effects of not living in this way. 'This sort of dreaming existence is the best. He who quits it to go in search of realities generally barters repose for repeated disappointments and vain regrets. His time, thoughts, and feelings are no longer at his own disposal. From that instant he does not survey the objects of nature as they are in themselves, but looks asquint at them to see whether he cannot make them the instruments of his ambition, interest, or pleasure; from a candid, undesigning, undisguised simplicity of character, his views become jaundiced, sinister, and double; he takes no further interest in the great changes of the world but as he has a paltry share in producing them; instead of opening his senses, his understanding, and his heart to the resplendent fabric of the universe, he holds a crooked mirror before his face, in which he may admire his own person and pretensions, and just glance his eye aside to see whether others are not admiring him too.'[1] This was not the kind of existence Hazlitt wanted, and in these years of reflection he learnt to reject it utterly. As if he knew his future

[1] 'On Living to One's-Self'.

work would depend on this slow deepening of his experience, he occupied himself with painting, that most contemplative of arts, and he later celebrated it in a fine essay. 'In writing, you have to contend with the world; in painting, you have only to carry on a friendly strife with Nature. From the moment that you take up the pencil, and look Nature in the face, you are at peace with your own heart. No angry passions rise to disturb the silent progress of the work, to shake the hand, or dim the brow: no irritable humours are set afloat: you have no absurd opinions to combat, no point to strain, no adversary to crush, no fool to annoy – you are actuated by fear or favour to no man. These is "no juggling here", no sophistry, no intrigue, no tampering with the evidence, no attempt to make black white, or white black: but you resign yourself into the hands of greater power, that of Nature, with the simplicity of a child, and the devotion of an enthusiast – "study with joy her manner, and with rapture taste her style". The mind is calm, and full at the same time. The hand and eye are equally employed. In tracing the commonest object, a plant or the stump of a tree, you learn something every moment ... Patience grows out of the endless pursuit, and turns it into a luxury. A streak in a flower, a wrinkle in a leaf, a tinge in a cloud, a stain in an old wall or ruin grey, are seized with avidity as the *spolia optima* of this sort of mental warfare, and furnish out labour for another half-day. The hours pass away untold, without chagrin, and without weariness; nor would you ever wish to pass them otherwise.'[1]

Hazlitt was never a good painter, and when he came to take his painting more seriously, no doubt these advantages lost their power to charm him. It is interesting to compare the intensity with which he pursued this craft and the disappointment he felt at his failure, with his careless attitude to his writing; it was as though he stumbled into his late and real profession by chance and against his will. 'I have not much pleasure in writing these *Essays*,' he wrote, 'or in reading them afterwards; though I own I now and then meet with a phrase that I like, or a thought that strikes me as a true one. But after I begin them, I am only anxious to get to the end of them, which I am not sure I shall do, for I seldom see my way a page or even a sentence beforehand; and when I have as by a miracle escaped, I trouble myself little more about them ... I

[1] 'On the Pleasure of Painting'.

have more satisfaction in my own thoughts than in dictating them to others; words are necessary to explain the impression of certain things upon me to the reader, but they rather weaken and draw a veil over than strengthen it to myself ... After I have once written on a subject, it goes out of my mind: my feelings about it have been melted down into words, and *then* I forget. I have, as it were, discharged my memory of its old habitual reckoning, and rubbed out the score of real sentiment. For the future it exists only for the sake of others – But I cannot say, from my own experience, that the same process takes place in transferring our ideas to canvas; they gain more than they lose in the mechanical transformation. One is never tired of painting, because you have to set down not what you knew already, but what you have just discovered.'[1]

In those same years (when Hazlitt 'still hoped to become a painter. I could not satisfy myself with what I did, yet the pain of failure had not yet stiffened anguish'), he studied deeply. His 'grand resort' at that period of his life was 'that branch of the tree of the knowledge of good and evil' which he called metaphysical reasoning. 'The study of metaphysics has this advantage at least – it promotes a certain integrity and uprightness of understanding, which is a cure for the spirit of lying.' And elsewhere he wrote: 'If it should be asked what use such studies are of, we might answer with Hume, perhaps of none, except that there are certain persons who find more entertainment in them than in any other.'[2]

He was a hermit, living mostly in the country, defending his solitude. When we have to reproach careless, unsociable and moody young men, we ought to remember Hazlitt, even though it is long odds against any one of them becoming a great writer. His astonishing mastery of his art in his maturity, when he was capable of writing a brilliant essay of several thousand words at a sitting and apparently without effort, has its roots in this seemingly confused and profitless period, when he was a painter who despaired of his painting, a metaphysician who could not find the right words for his ideas.

As this was the time when his character was formed, and he changed little afterwards, now we had better consider the man. He was of medium height, not strongly built but capable of great exertion (he walked enormous distances), with thick dark hair,

[1] 'On the Pleasure of Painting'.
[2] 'Characteristics. Mind and Motive'.

well-marked features, eyes that often seemed vague and shifting but that could blaze with enthusiasm or anger. He would often remain silent, almost sullen, in company, but on occasion with people he liked, could talk brilliantly, more or less as he wrote. (Indeed, his best essays are a kind of super-brilliant talk.) He was intensely introverted, at once shy and passionate, which explains the hang-dog effect he created in many companies. Lamb's early biographer, Thomas Talfourd, knew Hazlitt quite well after 1815 and described him vividly as he was during the last fifteen years of his life. 'His countenance was then handsome, but marked by a painful expression; his black hair, which had curled stiffly over his temples, had scarcely received its first tints of gray; his gait was awkward; his dress was neglected; and, in the company of strangers, his bashfulness was almost painful, – but when, in the society of Lamb and one or two others, he talked on his favourite themes of old English books, or old Italian pictures, no one's conversation would be more delightful ... When he mastered his diffidence, he did not talk for effect, to dazzle, or surprise, or annoy, but with the most simple and honest desire to make his view of the subject in hand entirely apprehended by his hearer. There was sometimes an obvious struggle to do this to his own satisfaction: he seemed labouring to drag his thought to light from its deep lurking-place; and, with timid distrust of that power of expression which he had found so late in life, he often betrayed a fear lest he had failed to make himself understood, and recurred to the subject again and again, that he might be assured he had succeeded.' More than ten years earlier, in 1803, when Hazlitt was still struggling to find his own voice, Coleridge conveyed him even more sharply. 'William Hazlitt', he wrote in a letter, 'is a thinking, observant, original man ... he has no imaginative memory. So much for his intellectuals. His manners are to 99 in 100 singularly repulsive; brow-hanging, shoe-contemplative, strange ... He is, I verily believe, kindly-natured; is very fond of, attentive to, and patient with, children, but he is jealous, gloomy and of an irritable pride ... With all this, there is much good in him. He is disinterested, an enthusiastic lover of the great men who have been before us; he says things that are his own, in a way of his own; and though from habitual shyness, and the outside and bearskin at least, of misanthropy, he is strangely confused and dark in his conversation, and delivers himself of almost all his conceptions with a Forceps, yet he says more than any man I ever knew that is his own in a way of his own; and oftentimes when he has warmed his mind, and the synovial juice has come out and spread over his joints, he will gallop for half an hour together with real eloquence.'[1]

IV

Alongside that failure of the French Revolution, which seemed to him to quench the promise and joy of youth, must be set his own failure with women. He was a deeply susceptible man and one capable of establishing on all levels a satisfying relationship with the right woman, but he never found her (or was always defeated in an early stage by his company manner). He made one marriage, with Sarah Stoddart, that was unfortunate; another, with Mrs Bridgewater, that was ridiculous; was crazily infatuated (a fine example of *anima* projection, Jungians please note) for almost half his forties with his landlady's daughter, Sarah Walker, a sly minx, and had to content himself as best he could with easily outraged village maidens or later with Covent Garden whores.

This long frustration threw into high relief those intense moments of pleasure and joy – and he has an unusual capacity for both – that he celebrates in his essays. He may be writing on a subject far removed from such a moment, but suddenly his remembrance of it will be there, glowing like some great jewel. He is at once the essayist of inspired common sense, the shrewdest insight, and of remembered impassioned enjoyment.

So, sketching and painting, brooding and inwardly philosophizing, Hazlitt roamed about that wonderful England of which we still catch a glimpse in the work of the old water-colourists. He wanted no more education: 'Anyone who has passed through the regular gradations of a classical education and is not made a fool by it, may consider himself as having had a very narrow escape.' Though capable at times of great bouts of reading, he was never a bookish man, and was most unlike that early Establishment figure, Sir James Mackintosh, of whom Hazlitt wrote: 'Sir James is one of those who see nature through the spectacle of books. He might like

[1] Samuel Taylor Coleridge to Thomas Wedgwood, letter of 16 September 1803), quoted in *The Life of William Hazlitt* by P. P. Howe (1922; rev. ed. 1947), pages 68–9.

to read an account of India; but India itself with its burning, shining face would be a mere blank, and endless waste to him. To persons of this class of mind things must be translated into words, visible images into abstract propositions, to meet their refined apprehensions; and they have no more to say to a matter-of-fact staring them in the face without a label on its mouth, than they would to a hippopotamus.'[1] Hazlitt was not of this class of mind; he liked to see things for himself. But, as we saw, he discovered that this life of wandering, sketching, and metaphysics 'meant taking a short cut to starvation'. After a few years divided between writing and painting, in 1812 he became Parliamentary Reporter for the *Morning Chronicle* and, a year later, its dramatic critic.

He had a great love of the theatre and a high opinion of its value. 'Wherever there is a playhouse', he wrote in 1817, 'the world will go on not amiss. The stage not only refines the manners, but it is the best teacher of morals, for it is the truest and most intelligible picture of life. It stamps the image of virtue on the mind by first softening the rude materials of which it is composed, by a sense of pleasure. It regulates the passions by giving a loose to the imagination. It points out the selfish and depraved to our detestation; the amiable and generous to our admiration; and if it clothes the more seductive vices with the borrowed graces of wit and fancy, even those graces operate as a diversion to the coarser poison of experience and bad example, and often prevent or carry off the infection by inoculating the mind with a certain taste and elegance.'[2]

When he began writing about the theatre, Hazlitt was just in time to salute the genius of Edmund Kean, who owed much to his enthusiastic notices. Years later, when Kean was being hooted off the stage, Hazlitt made a one-man cavalry charge at the mob: 'Let a great man but "fall into misfortunes" and then you discover the real dispositions of the loving public towards their pretended idol. See how they set upon him the moment he is down, how they watch for the smallest slip, the first pretext to pick a quarrel with him, how slow they are to acknowledge any worth, how quick to exaggerate an error, how ready to trample upon and tear "to tatters, to very rags" the frailties which being flesh and blood he

[1] Sir James Mackintosh, in *The Spirit of the Age.*
[2] 'On Actors and Acting'.

has in common with all men, while yet they overlook or malign the incomparable excellence which they can neither reach nor find a substitute for ... It was not the adulterer they pelted with stones – as to that, which of them that was not a lying knave and a hypocrite could lay hand to heart and claim the right to pick up the first stone? – but the man who bore on his brow the mark of the fire from Heaven.'

But this was written when Hazlitt was fifty, only two years before his death, and by that time he could look back not only on so much work wonderfully well done, on the friendship of Lamb and Keats (who greatly admired him), but also on an unceasing torrent of abuse. The Establishment of the period may not have employed as many hacks as it has since acquired, but their virulence was appalling. He was 'the pimpled Hazlitt' (though he had in fact a clear, pale face), 'an angry buffoon', 'an unprincipled blunderer', and *Blackwood's Magazine* announced that 'the day is perhaps not far distant when the Charlatan shall be stripped to the naked skin, and made to swallow his own vile prescriptions'. Over many years that same magazine conducted against Hazlitt a campaign of fearful vilification. In one issue Wilson spoke of 'that wild, blackbill Hazlitt. You do not, I perceive, know what a paltry creature this is, otherwise you would either have said more or less about him than you have done ... He is a mere quack, Mr Editor, and a mere bookmaker; one of the sort that lounge in third-rate bookshops, and write third-rate books.' On one occasion he figures as ' a small fetid, blear-eyed pug'; on another (referring to the *Liber Amoris*) as 'an acknowledged scamp of the lowest order – a scamp by his own confession steeped in ignorance and malice of his very ribald lips'. This relentless and bitterly personal campaign ended only with his death, which *Blackwood's* saw fit to pass without noticing. A critic in 1854 summarized it thus: 'Wilson and Lockhart bent all their young power against a writer whom both in their hearts admired, and from whom both had learned much. The first twenty-five volumes of *Blackwood's Magazine* are disgraced by incessant, furious, and scurrilous attacks upon the person, private character, talents, and moral and religious principles of Hazlitt, which future ages shall regard with wonder and disgust.'

Later critics like Leslie Stephen, Saintsbury, Birrell, while admitting the force and brilliance of Hazlitt's writing, were inclined to shake their heads over his passionate prejudices and truculence; but they had never had to suffer this kind of abuse while writing against the clock and the bailiff. That Hazlitt was an awkward, difficult fellow must be admitted. But he held unpopular opinions, believing that the poor were undeservedly wretched, that the triumph of reaction after 1815 was a disaster, that many glittering public figures were windbags and humbugs; he detested and unmasked stupidity and hypocrisy; he insisted upon telling the truth as he saw it; and this was no way then, just as it is not now, to win friends and influence people. No sinecures, no pensions, came his way. On his deathbed he asked Jeffrey, for whom he had often written in the *Edinburgh Review*, to send him ten pounds. Jeffrey, so Carlyle records, sent him fifty.

Most of his contemporaries he alienated, and most of them attacked him either in the public press or in private communications. Wordsworth, for example, whom Hazlitt so deeply admired in his youth, froze at once in any company that also contained Hazlitt. And he could write, as he did to Haydon in 1817: 'The miscreant Hazlitt continues, I have heard, his abuse of Southey, Coleridge and myself, in the *Examiner*. I hope that you do not associate with the fellow; he is not a proper person to be admitted into respectable society.' And Coleridge remained so unforgiving as to produce the following epitaph:

Obiit Saturday, Sept 18, 1830
W. H. *Eheu*!
Beneath this stone does William Hazlitt lie,
Thankless of all that God or man could give,
He lived like one who never thought to die,
He died like one who dared not hope to live.

The reasons for such unappeasable hostility may be found in Hazlitt's frequent sidelights on himself in the Essays. In one of the most important he wrote: 'Many people boast of being masters in their own house. I pretend to be master of my own mind. I should be sorry to have an ejectment served upon me for any notions I may choose to entertain there. Within that little circle I would fain be an absolute monarch ... I am not to be browbeat or wheedled out of any of my settled convictions. Opinion to opinion, I will face any man. Prejudice, fashion, the cant of the moment, go for nothing; and as for the reason of the thing, it can only be supposed to rest with me or another, in proportion to the pains we have taken to ascertain it. Where the pursuit of truth has been the habitual study of any man's life, the love of truth will be his ruling passion . . . If "to be wise were to be obstinate", I might set up for as great a philosopher as the best of them; for some of my conclusions are as fixed and as incorrigible to proof as need be. I am attached to them in consequence of the pains, and anxiety, and the waste of time they have cost me. In fact, I should not well know what to do without them at this time of day; nor how to get others to supply their place. I would quarrel with the best friend I have sooner than acknowledge the absolute right of the Bourbons.' Few people have the strength to tolerate such firm refusal to compromise. As a contemporary very fairly stated the case in the *Edinburgh Review*: 'If Mr Hazlitt has not generally met with impartial justice from his contemporaries, we must say that he has himself partly to blame. Some of the attacks of which he has been the object, have no doubt been purely brutal and malignant; but others have, in a great measure, arisen from feeling of which he has unwisely set the example. His seeming carelessness of that public opinion which he would influence – his love of startling paradoxes – and his intrusion of political virulence, at seasons when the mind is prepared only for the delicate investigations of taste, have naturally provoked a good deal of asperity, and prevented the due appreciation of his powers.'

Quarrels even cast a shadow over his relations with Lamb, perhaps his staunchest friend. In 1816 Lamb described a piece which Hazlitt had written about him as 'a pretty compendium of observation, which the author has collected in my disparagement, from some hundreds of social evenings which we had spent together – however in spite of all, there is something tough in my attachment to H., which these violent strainings cannot quite dislocate or sever asunder. I get no conversation in London that is absolutely worth attending to but his.' And Hazlitt himself conveys the delight of those hundreds of social evenings in his essay 'On the Conversation of Authors': 'When a set of adepts, of *illuminati*, get about a question, it is worth while to hear them talk. They may snarl and quarrel over it, like dogs; but they pick it bare to the bone, they masticate it thoroughly . . . This was the case formerly at L[amb]'s – where we used to have many lively skirmishes at their Thursday evening parties . . . There was L[amb] himself, the most delightful, the most provoking, the most witty and sensible of men. He always made the best pun, and the best remark in the course of the evening. His serious conversation, like his serious writing, is the best. No one ever stammered out such fine, piquant, deep, eloquent things in half a dozen half sentences as he does. His jests scald like tears: and he probes a question with a play upon words. What a keen laughing, hair-brained vein of homefelt truth! What choice venom! How often did we cut into the haunch of letters, while we discussed the haunch of mutton on the table! How we skimmed the cream of criticism! How we got into the heart of controversy! How we picked out the marrow of authors!'

V

It might be said that these discursive critical evenings with Lamb served Hazlitt well later on, for though he is more an intensely personal essayist than a critic proper, his critical insights were extraordinarily keen and just, the best of his time. He might quarrel with Wordsworth and Coleridge, but in spite of his passionate prejudices he understood and praised their poetry. He regarded the former as 'the most original poet now living ... His poetry is not external, but internal; it does not depend upon tradition, or story, or old song; he furnishes it from his own mind, and is his own subject. He is the poet of mere sentiment ... His poems open a finer and deeper vein of thought and feeling than any poet in modern times has done, or attempted. He has produced a deeper impression, and on a smaller circle, than any other of his contemporaries. His powers have been mistaken by the age, nor does he exactly understand them himself. He cannot form a whole. He has not the constructive faculty. He can give only the fine tones of thought, drawn from his mind by accident or nature, like the sounds drawn from the Aeolian harp by the wandering gale. He is totally deficient in all the machinery of poetry. His *Excursion*, taken as a whole, notwithstanding the noble materials thrown away in it, is a proof of this. The line labours, the sentiment moves slow; but the poem stands stock-still.' And again: his poetry 'is one of the innovations of the time. It partakes of, and is carried along with, the revolutionary movement of our age: the political changes of the day were the model on which he formed and conducted his poetical experiments. His Muse (it cannot be denied and without this we cannot explain its character at all) is a levelling one. It proceeds on a principle of equality, and strives to reduce all things to the same standard. It is distinguished by a proud humility. It relies upon its own resources, and disdains external show and relief. It takes the commonest events and objects, as a test to prove that nature is always interesting from its inherent truth and beauty, without any of the ornaments of dress or pomp of circumstances to set it off. Hence the unaccountable mixture of seeming simplicity and real abstruseness in the *Lyrical Ballads*. Fools have laughed at, wise men scarcely understand, them. He takes a subject or a story merely as pegs or loops to hang thought and feeling on; the incidents are trifling, in proportion to his contempt for imposing appearances; the reflections are profound, according to the gravity and aspiring pretensions of his mind.'[1]

When sound gentlemanly Tories like Lockhart were dismissing the poetry of Keats as 'drivelling idiocy' and the poet himself as 'a starved apothecary', Hazlitt admired the work and befriended the man; indeed their friendship, though it lasted far too short a time, must have been a source of great solace to Hazlitt, for the poet was one of his greatest admirers. His respect was such that he could write in 1818: 'Hazlitt has damned the bigotted and blue-stockinged; how durst the Man? He is your only good damner, and if ever I am damn'd – damn me if I shouldn't like him to damn me'. On the other hand Hazlitt did not much care for Shelley, in spite of their common republican views; but it can hardly be denied that his criticism of that poet does reveal certain enduring faults. 'He is clogged by no dull system of realities, no earth-bound feelings, no rooted prejudices, by nothing that belongs to the mighty trunk and hard husk of nature and habit, but is drawn up by irresistible levity to the regions of mere speculation and fancy, to the sphere of air and fire, where his delighted spirit floats in "seas of pearl and clouds of amber" ... Bubbles are to him the only realities – touch them and they vanish ... Though a man in knowledge, he is a child in feeling.'[2]

Very often, in the course of his criticism of others, Hazlitt spoke perhaps unconsciously of himself. In his study of Coleridge there

[1] Mr Wordsworth, in *The Spirit of the Age*.

[2] Quoted in *The Life of William Hazlitt* by P. P. Howe (1922; rev. ed. 1947), pages 227–8.

is a passage worth quoting which well describes the casual element, the lack of driving force, the absence of direction, in his life. 'Persons of the greatest capacity', he wrote, 'are often those, who for this reason do the least; for surveying themselves from the highest point of view, amidst the infinite variety of the universe, their own share in it seems trifling, and scarce worth a thought; and they prefer the contemplation of all that is, or has been, or can be, to the making a coil about doing what, when done, is no better than vanity. It is hard to concentrate all our attention and efforts on one pursuit, except from ignorance of others; and without this concentration of our faculties no great progress can be made in any one thing. It is not merely that that mind is not capable of the effort; it does not think the effort worth making. Action is one; but thought is manifold. He whose restless eye glances through the wide compass of nature and art, will not consent to have "his own nothings monstered"; but he must do this before he can give his whole soul to them. The mind, after "letting contemplation have its fill" or:

> Sailing with supreme dominion
> Through the azure deep of air,

sinks down on the ground, breathless, exhausted, powerless, inactive; or if it must have some vent to its feelings, seeks the most easy and obvious; is soothed by friendly flattery, lulled by the murmur of immediate applause: thinks as it were, aloud, and babbles in its dreams!'[1]

The best of Hazlitt's criticism is to be found in his *Lectures on the English Comic Writers,* first published in 1819, and in one of his later works, an original that has since produced many inferior imitations, *The Spirit of the Age, or Contemporary Portraits.* When so many of his distinguished contemporaries were lashing out at Hazlitt in phrases that were to endure, it comes as a surprise to find evidence of the high esteem in which he was held as a critic appearing in the newspapers of the time. At the end of his course of lectures on the Comic Writers, the *Morning Chronicle,* no doubt supported by the majority of his audience, said that his reputation as a critic 'stood already high with the public; but we are mistaken if these Lectures will not add to it. He displayed the same boldness and originality of thinking; the same critical acuteness,

[1] Coleridge, in *Lectures on the English Poets.*

eloquence and felicity of expression for which his Lectures on the Poets were so eminently distinguished.' And, we might add to this catalogue, a deep understanding of the nature not only of wit and humour but of life itself. For the Hazlitt of the warmly intimate Essays always overlapped the critical Hazlitt, and his Lectures are as much about life as about literature.

In *The Spirit of the Age*, among many good things, may be found – a dried pressed thistle – what is left of Gifford, who with his anonymous assassins of the *Quarterly Review* had so often attacked Hazlitt and had almost murdered Keats: 'The *Quarterly Review*, besides the political tirades and denunciations of suspected writers, intended for the guidance of the heads of families, is filled up with accounts of books of Voyages and Travels for the amusement of the younger branches. The poetical department is almost a sinecure, consisting of mere summary decisions and a list of quotations. Mr Croker is understood to contribute the St Helena articles and the liberality, Mr Canning the practical good sense, Mr D'Israeli the good nature, Mr Jacob the modesty, Mr Southey the consistency, and the Editor himself the chivalrous spirit and the attacks on Lady Morgan.'[1] As Walter Raleigh said of Hazlitt: 'He came of a tough stock, and fighting blood tingled in his veins.' It was probably this fighting blood, combined with his taste for solitude, which enabled him to enjoy such a detached view of the literary and political scene of his time. And, as an example will show, his opinions have lost nothing of their sharpness and relevance; he might be writing today when he says that 'we have lost the art of reading, or the privilege of writing, voluminously, since the days of Addison. Learning no longer weaves the interminable page with patient drudgery, nor ignorance pores over it with implicit faith. As authors multiply in number, books diminish in size; we cannot now, as formerly, swallow libraries whole in a single folio: solid quarto has given place to slender duodecimo, and the dingy letterpress contracts its dimensions, and retreats before the white, unsullied, faultless margin. Modern authorship is become a species of stenography: we contrive even to read by proxy. We skim the cream of prose without any trouble; we get at the quintessence of poetry without loss of time. The staple commodity, the coarse, heavy, dirty,

[1] Mr Gifford, in *The Spirit of the Age*.

unwieldy bullion of books, is driven out of the market of learning, and the intercourse of the literary world is carried on, and the credit of the great capitalists sustained, by the flimsy circulating medium of magazines and reviews. Those who are chiefly concerned in catering for the taste of others, and serving up critical opinions in compendious, elegant, and portable form, are not forgetful of themselves: they are not scrupulously solicitous, idly inquisitive about the real merits, the *bona fide* contents of the works they are deputed to appraise and value, any more than the reading public who employ them. They look no farther for the contents of the work than the title-page, and pronounce a peremptory decision on its merits or defects by a glance at the name and party of the writer.'

The great essays of his maturity – 'On People With One Idea', 'The Indian Jugglers', 'The Flight', 'On going a Journey', 'On the Fear of Death', and the rest – were mostly written either at Winterslow, on Salisbury Plain, which makes a frequent appearance in his essays, or in various lodgings in London. There he rose late, sat drinking his horrible strong tea (he had forsworn alcohol because he thought it bad for his stomach, but in the end the tea did him more harm) until evening, and if he had an essay to write – which usually meant that he needed the money – composed it in an incredibly short time, with hardly a correction. That he enjoyed this modest routine cannot be doubted. In his last full year of life he wrote: 'Taking one thing with another, I have no great cause to complain. If I had been a merchant, a bookseller, or the proprietor of a newspaper, instead of what I am, I might have had more money or possessed a town and country house, instead of lodging in a first or second floor, as it may happen. But what then? I see how the man of business and fortune passes his time. He is up and in the city by eight, swallows his breakfast in haste, attends a meeting of creditors, must read Lloyd's lists, consult the price of consols, study the markets, look into his accounts, pay his workmen, and superintend his clerks: he has hardly a minute in the day to himself, and perhaps in the four-and-twenty hours does not do a single thing that he would do if he could help it. Surely, this sacrifice of time and inclination requires some compensation, which it meets with. But how am I entitled to make my fortune (which cannot be done without all this anxiety and drudgery) who hardly do any thing at all, and never any thing but what I like to do? I rise when I please, breakfast *at length*, write what comes into my head, and after taking a mutton-chop and a dish of strong tea, go to the play, and thus my time passes. Mr —— has no time to go to the play. It was but the other day that I had to get up a little earlier than usual to go into the city about some money transaction, which appeared to me a prodigious hardship: if so, it was plain that I must lead a tolerably easy life: nor should I object to passing mine over again.'

Hazlitt's essays are not faultless. There are too many references to the dawn of the Revolution, the apostasy of the Lake Poets, scurrilous Tory critics, and various personal matters. When the style fails to achieve a flashing poetry of phrase, it is content with an easy romantic lushness – 'The dew from a thousand pastures was gathered into its softness.' Too often he luxuriates in his moods, abandons himself too abjectly. But the manly sense and wit return; the truth is spoken; and as his heart warms to the remembrance of pleasure, happiness, glory, the prose glows with rich imagery: 'We walk though life, as through a narrow path, with a thin curtain drawn around it; behind are ranged rich portraits, airy harps are strung – yet we will not stretch forth our hands and lift aside the veil, to catch glimpses of the one or sweep the chords of the other. As in a theatre, when the old-fashion green curtain drew up, groups of figures, fantastic dresses, laughing faces, rich banquets, stately columns, gleaming vistas, appeared beyond, so we have only at any time to "peep through the blanket of the past" to possess ourselves at once of all that has regaled our senses, that is stored up in our memory, that has struck our fancy, that has pierced our hearts: yet to all this we are indifferent, insensible, and seem intent only on the present vexation, the future disappointment.' So here, in 'A Farewell to Essay-writing', he seems to anticipate Proust's *Time Regained*.

VII

It is not easy to write like Hazlitt. As he wrote himself in an essay which perfectly summarized as well as exemplified his own approach to prose: 'It is not easy to write a familiar style. Many people mistake a familiar for a vulgar style, and suppose that to write without affectation is to write at random. On the contrary, there is nothing that requires more precision, and, if I may so say, purity of expression, than the style I am speaking of. It utterly rejects not only all unmeaning pomp, but all low, cant phrases, and loose, unconnected, *slipshod* allusions. It is not to take the first word that offers, but the best word in common use; it is not to throw words together in any combinations we please, but to follow and avail ourselves of the true idiom of the language. To write a genuine familiar or truly English style, is to write as anyone would speak in common conversation who had a thorough command and choice of words, or who could discourse with ease, force, and perspicuity, setting aside all pedantic and oratorical flourishes . . . It is easy to affect a pompous style, to use a word twice as big as the thing you want to express: it is not so easy to pitch upon the very word that exactly fits it. Out of eight or ten words equally common, equally intelligible, with nearly equal pretensions, it is a matter of some nicety and discrimination to pick out the very one the preferableness of which is scarcely perceptible, but decisive.'[1]

Hazlitt remains, to my mind, the supreme essayist for young men, bent on writing themselves, to study and to devour. A course of him might be prescribed for those young writers, clever, not dishonest, but altogether too dubious and fearful, who consider anything too far removed from saloon-bar talk and boiled cabbage and washing-up to be 'phoney'. He could give them a lift they badly need. And much of what he said needs saying even more urgently today. 'Happy are they who live in the dream of their own existence, and see all things in the light of their own minds; who walk by faith and hope; to whom the guiding star of their youth still shines from afar, and into whom the spirit of the world has not entered! They have not been "hurt by the archers", nor has the iron entered their souls. The world has no hand on them.'[2]

Here our 'angry young men' can find a man who knew what he had to be angry about, and yet, throughout a life harrowed by ill luck, poverty, toil, insult and calumny, a man who celebrated with gratitude and joy every intense moment that pierced the heart and irradiated the mind.

[1] 'On Familiar Style'.
[2] Mind and Motive'.

Biographical Critic and Man of Passion

R. L. Brett

Those who dislike biographical criticism and maintain that an author's life is irrelevant to his writings will find it difficult to come to terms with Hazlitt. For Hazlitt was a biographical critic who believed that ideas are best seen as an expression of personality. For him character was always more important than abstract notions. Even when dealing with fictional writing his preoccupation with people manifests itself. His criticism of Shakespeare concentrates on character, and in *The Dramatic Literature of the Age of Elizabeth* he expresses a dislike of the 'German' type of tragedy as compared with Shakespeare's, because its characters are merely 'mouth-pieces', the symbolization of 'speculative opinions' and not flesh and blood people with a life of their own. Not only was Hazlitt a great exponent of biographical criticism, but nearly all his writing is autobiographical and personal, recording his opinions, airing his prejudices, expressing his likes and dislikes, and defending his views. Above all, he advances with passionate conviction what he himself believes to be true and demolishes what he thinks is false. He is a master of rhetoric whose task, as he sees it, is not only to please his readers, but to persuade them, to convince them, and to rouse them. Ideas are not so much a matter of intellectual assent but of how we live.

This means that his writing was often argumentative, a quality strengthened by the realization that most of his contemporaries disliked him and by a determination to command their attention and respect, even if he could not win their affection. There is often in his writing the feeling that he is an outsider, a sense at times of injured merit, though to do Hazlitt justice, later generations have acknowledged his merit and recognized that he was treated unfairly in his own day. One can discern the seeds of this sense of alienation in Hazlitt's upbringing. His father was a Unitarian minister and he was educated at a Unitarian academy. To be a Unitarian at this time was more than a matter of religious opinion; it meant that one was a radical in politics, probably with republican sympathies, an enemy of the aristocracy and of the Established Church with its state patronage and traditional privileges. Those who held these views naturally supported the French Revolution, and it was Hazlitt's unswerving allegiance to this cause which increasingly isolated him from popular opinion in England. He once told Coleridge that he had not changed any of his opinions since the age of sixteen. Coleridge, who had been an ardent supporter of the Revolution as a young man, retorted, 'Why then, you are no wiser now than you were then!', and his reply indicates how public sentiment had shifted during their lifetime. To understand this more clearly we must turn to the details of Hazlitt's birth and education.

William Hazlitt was born in 1778 at Maidstone in Kent. His father was a dreamer rather than a man of action, taken up with theological speculation and disputes concerning religious and civic liberty, but Hazlitt always loved him for his piety and unworldliness. After moving to Ireland the family left in 1783 for America: there Hazlitt's father thought he might find a more congenial atmosphere than at home, where his sympathy for the American colonists was looked at askance and where he felt a lack of freedom. But experience dashed these hopes. After four years of disappointment and illness, the family returned to England and settled in the little town of Wem in Shropshire, where the elder Hazlitt became minister of the Unitarian congregation. The quiet simplicity of his home at Wem, with its emotional security and firm radical principles, remained with Hazlitt throughout a turbulent life as a memory to sustain and console him. His first departure from home came in his fifteenth year when he was sent to New College, Hackney, an academy which trained candidates for the ministry.

Hazlitt entered New College in 1793, the year in which the British Government declared war against France. The declaration came as a profound shock to him. He had grown up in circles which welcomed the Revolution; his father's distinguished friends, Richard Price and Joseph Priestley, the intellectual and spiritual luminaries of the Unitarians, had both defended the Revolution, not only on philosophical and political grounds but as the expression of God's purposes in history. The tradition in which he had been nurtured saw the history of the previous hundred years as a great movement of ideas and events which had started with the revolution of 1688, had led to the demand for American independence and had given birth to the French Revolution. Dr Price, in his *Discourse on the Love of our Country*, delivered on 4 November 1789, at the Meeting House in the Old Jewry in London, had welcomed the events in France with an apocalyptic fervour and discerned in them the realization of his millenarian hopes. 'After sharing in the benefits of one Revolution', he declared, 'I have been spared to be a witness of two other Revolutions, both glorious. And now methinks, I see the ardour for liberty catching and spreading; a general amendment beginning in human affairs; the dominion of kings changed for the dominion of laws, and the dominion of priests giving way to the dominion of reason and conscience.' Those of Hazlitt's generation, at least those of spirit and generous impulses, could say with Wordsworth, 'Bliss was it in that dawn to be alive, But to be young was very heaven'. Looking back at this period in 'On the Feeling of Immortality in Youth', Hazlitt was to write:

> For my part, I set out in life with the French Revolution, and that event had considerable influence on my early feelings, as on those of others. Youth then was doubly such. It was the dawn of a new era, a new impulse had been given to men's minds, and the sun of Liberty rose upon the sun of Life in the same day, and both were proud to run their race together. Little did I dream, while my first hopes and wishes went hand in hand with those of the human race, that long before my eyes should close, that dawn would be overcast, and set once more in the night of despotism.

Hazlitt's disillusionment was profound and in some ways permanent, but its first consequence was its unsettling effect upon his career at the Hackney academy. Even without the pressure of great events Hazlitt would probably have been unsettled, for the college was renowned for its free-thinking, and the prescribed courses of study did not come easily to him. It is no wonder, perhaps, that a boy of his years and in such circumstances should find it difficult to retain his Christian faith. After three years at Hackney Hazlitt left, minus his faith and determined not to enter the ministry. There followed a period at Wem spent in desultory reading when he had no definite career in mind, and this was brought to an end only in 1798 when Hazlitt met Coleridge for the first time and realized that he had reached a turning point in his life.

The account of their meeting is told in 'My First Acquaintance with Poets', the eloquence of which witnesses to the effect Coleridge had on Hazlitt as a young man of nineteen. Coleridge at this time was a neighbour of William and Dorothy Wordsworth in the Quantock Hills,[1] and the two poets were engaged in writing and compiling the poems which were to appear at the end of the year as *Lyrical Ballads*. Coleridge, without any prospect of a secure income, was considering entering the Unitarian ministry and had travelled to Shrewsbury to preach a trial sermon before the congregation there. Hazlitt describes graphically Coleridge's appearance in the pulpit and his announcement of the text, 'And he went up into the mountain to pray, HIMSELF, ALONE'. He was, of course, listening to the greatest talker of the age and Coleridge's mastery of language seemed to him 'like an eagle dallying with the wind'. 'Poetry and Philosophy had met together. Truth and Genius had embraced, under the eye and with the sanction of Religion.' As he walked back to Wem he viewed the landscape with a new enthusiasm, 'for there was a spirit of hope and youth in all nature, that turned every thing into good'. The next day Coleridge visited the elder Hazlitt and the young man was entranced by his conversation. He learned with disappointment that Coleridge, while at Shrewsbury, had received the offer of an annuity from the Wedgwoods and that this genius was not to become their neighbour after all. But he recovered when Coleridge invited him to visit Nether Stowey. The invitation was given in January, 1798, and the visit did not take place until May, but the delay did nothing to diminish the excitement and pleasure Hazlitt gained from his month's stay in the Quantocks. He was fascinated by Coleridge's wide-ranging mind and eloquence, and impressed with Wordsworth's personality and poetic power. They treated him as an equal and gave him a new self-confidence. He had entered a world in which poetry, politics,

[1] In Somerset.

philosophy, and psychology were the topics of everyday conversation and found the experience exhilarating. Indeed, although he did not realize it at the time, never were Hazlitt's relations with the two poets to be so cordial again.

The grounds of future discord lay partly in Hazlitt's awkward and touchy personality, but there were larger issues which were to divide them. These had their origins in the great shift of political opinion which was beginning to take place in England. While some saw in the French Revolution the realization of their dearest hopes, the majority looked across the Channel with mounting alarm. Already in 1790 Burke had published his *Reflections on the French Revolution* and had followed this in 1796 with his *Letter to a Noble Lord*. These works had a great influence in encouraging resistance to the Revolution and were all the more impressive since their author had sided with the cause of American independence. Burke argued that political institutions were not simply mechanical contrivances erected to serve the will of the people, to be scrapped and replaced according to some new blue-print of society, but that society develops by a principle of organic growth and that to tear down institutions is to risk anarchy. The swing of public opinion made even radical reform unpopular, and this was increased by the appearance in 1798 of Malthus's *Essay on the Principle of Population*.

Malthus's book argued with what seemed to be scientific irrefutability that reform was not only irrelevant but positively dangerous since 'a strong...check on population from the difficulty of subsistence' manifested in such forms as famine and disease was always inevitable. To upset the natural process of self preservation and to put benevolence in their place would be to meddle with the design of providence and to court disaster. Hazlitt's unstinted admiration of Burke as a prose stylist did little to modify his dislike of Burke's doctrines, and for Malthus he had nothing but contempt. Hazlitt's *Reply* to Malthus had to wait until 1807 when a new edition of the *Essay on Population* and Malthus's *Letter to Samuel Whitbread* both appeared, and then his attack on their author was savage in its abuse. Whitbread had brought a Poor Law Bill before Parliament and the spectacle of Malthus lobbying MPs in an attempt to abolish Poor Law Relief roused Hazlitt's fiercest anger. He preferred to believe with those, like Godwin, who argued that if only social institutions could be modified or new ones brought into being, human nature would respond and a just society could realize the dreams of the reformers. For him, society was made for man, not man for society.

Hazlitt spent the years from 1798 to 1803 trying to follow in the footsteps of his elder brother who was a painter. He studied first in London and then in Paris. When he arrived in Paris, England and France were at peace; when he left it in 1803, England was about to declare war again. The great majority of the English people supported the war, but again Hazlitt found himself in a dwindling minority. He saw the war as an attack on democracy, and during his time abroad he developed an affection for the French people and an admiration for their First Consul, Napoleon. These were grounds enough for the rift that was to open up between Hazlitt and Wordsworth and Coleridge, for the two poets now regarded the French Revolution as a god who had failed, but it was the personal element which was to make their quarrel especially acrimonious.

When he returned from France in 1803, Wordsworth and Coleridge were living with their families in the Lake District and Hazlitt joined them there in the following summer. He now saw himself as a portrait painter and this was how Coleridge wrote of him in a letter to Tom Wedgwood in September of that year. 'William Hazlitt is a thinking, observant, original man, of great power as a Painter of Character Portraits, and far more in the manner of the Old Painters, than any living Artist.' He was more experienced than the youth who had visited the Quantocks, but, even so, the picture Coleridge gives is that of an odd and immature character.

> His manners are to 99 in 100 singularly repulsive: brow-hanging, shoe-contemplative, *strange* ... he is, I verily believe, kindly-natured – is very fond of, attentive to, and patient with, children, but he is jealous, gloomy, and of an irritable Pride – and addicted to women, as objects of sexual Indulgence. With all this, there is much good in him ... he is strangely confused and dark in his conversation and delivers himself of almost all his conceptions with a Forceps, yet he says more than any man I ever knew ... He sends well-headed and well-feathered Thoughts straight forwards to the mark with a Twang of the Bow-string.

The two poets and their circle welcomed Hazlitt in their midst, but perhaps he felt they did not take him seriously enough. Though his talents as a painter were undeniable, the portraits he painted did not meet with unqualified praise. Dorothy Wordsworth, who always had a sharp tongue, told Lady Beaumont that the portrait of Coleridge made her think of the poet as 'not merely dying, but dying of sorrow and raised up upon his bed to take a last farewell of his Friends'. Southey, who had recently moved to Keswick, said of Wordsworth's portrait that it represented him 'At the gallows – deeply affected by his deserved fate – yet determined to die like a man'. But it was what Coleridge referred to in his letter as 'sexual Indulgence' which brought an ignominious end to Hazlitt's visit. The letters of both Wordsworth and Coleridge give details of the incident which caused Hazlitt to leave, and while they were written later and after Hazlitt had attacked their reputations, there is no reason to doubt their essential truth. Apparently Hazlitt attempted to assault sexually some of the local girls, and one attack in particular so incensed the community that the men chased him out of the village, from which he escaped over the hills in clothes and with money provided by either Coleridge or Wordsworth. In view of the revelations Hazlitt was to make later in *Liber Amoris* one can believe the substance of these accounts, for his personality reveals a man of great sexual passion, at once attracted to women and yet inhibited in their presence.

Following this debacle in the Lakes, Hazlitt's fortunes were at a low ebb and remained so for another eight years. After a retreat to Wem he ventured again on the literary scene in London and found true friends in Charles and Mary Lamb. The Lambs were the centre of a talented circle and at their Wednesday evening parties at Mitre Court Hazlitt was variously tolerated, encouraged, and approved of. For the Lambs themselves he retained an enduring affection. Many of his essays look back on the warmth of their friendship, and his portrait of Charles Lamb in the National Portrait Gallery remains as his best known painting and as a token of gratitude to one whose loyalty remained constant. It was through the Lambs that Hazlitt met in 1807 his first wife, Sarah Stoddart. She was the daughter of a retired naval officer who lived at Winterslow near Salisbury, and upon his death she had inherited a house of her own and a modest income of £80 a year. She was no longer young, for she was three years older than Hazlitt, and had already been involved in a number of unfortunate love affairs. What induced Hazlitt to marry her remains a mystery. She had many virtues, including common sense and practicality, but she lacked any grace of manner or appearance and, above all, the romantic sensibility which would have inspired Hazlitt and aroused him from his constitutional melancholy. She brought him a measure of financial security and provided him with a home he could call his own, but though he was used to living in the country and loved the Wiltshire landscape, he felt that his future lay in London. Even at the beginning he entered on married life with no enthusiasm and, as the years passed, viewed his choice of a wife as another of life's misfortunes. He embarked on marriage with the grim realization that he had failed as a painter and as a man of letters. In 1805 he had published *An Essay on the Principles of Human Action*, but it had been virtually ignored; he had some political essays to his credit, and a few commissioned works and more recently had written his *Reply* to Malthus, but none of them gave him much of a reputation. In 1809 he started to edit the Memoirs of the reformer Thomas Holcroft, who died in March of that year, but the work had a chequered history and did not appear until 1816. In 1812 he turned, as so many other indigent authors were doing, to the delivery of a series of lectures. These lectures on philosophy commanded little attention, but helped Hazlitt to clarify his own ideas and were useful to the tasks that lay ahead. In the same year he became parliamentary and dramatic reporter to the *Morning Chronicle* and now at long last found an occupation which matched his genius and which was to establish his career.

At first he was restricted to reporting Parliamentary debates from the press gallery, but soon began contributing short essays and occasional pieces which so pleased his editor that he became dramatic critic and literary reviewer After eighteen months' apprenticeship, brought to an end by political differences, he moved to the *Champion*, then the radical *Examiner* run by John and Leigh Hunt, and finally the *Times*. As a young man he had wrestled with words and found every piece of writing an agonizing process of making his ideas articulate, but now the pressure of working to a deadline and having to deal with current events seemed to have a liberating effect upon him, and the six years he spent with these journals saw a tremendous output of writing on politics, philosophy, the theatre, art, literature, and *belles lettres*. His contributions to 'The Round Table', a feature of the *Examiner*, gave him a freedom to develop the essay form in his own characteristic manner, especially to compound literature, politics, and personalities. His new-found confidence charged these pieces with great energy and gave them what he believed was the hallmark of great art, the quality he called 'gusto'. He also adopted a procedure which he was to use with increasing success; this was to cream off the best of his journalism, and to publish it later in book form. From his essays in the *Examiner* and elsewhere he gathered together the essays which appeared as *The Round Table* and some of the material which went to the making of his *Characters of Shakespeare's Plays*, and when he left the *Times* produced *A View of the English Stage* and *Political Essays*.

Hazlitt's attacks on Wordsworth, Coleridge and Southey, whom he now regarded as renegades, and on the Tory politicians were venomous in tone and, as was to be expected, were answered in kind. The *Quarterly Review* and *Blackwood's Magazine* were quick in their condemnation, and the latter in particular mounted a sustained campaign against him, but Hazlitt thrived on opposition and his style became stronger with debate. The passion that informed his language sprang from a deeply held conviction that after 1815 the cause of political reform was lost, that the government was no more than a parcel of hypocrites and knaves who had little sense of justice and lacked even compassion for the poor and oppressed. His style may often have been vituperative and his arguments prejudiced, but the same could be said of his opponents, and *Blackwood's* in particular descended to the level of abusing not only his character but his personal appearance. Public contention spurred Hazlitt to new levels of achievement and improved his prospects by bringing him into a closer association with the *Edinburgh Review* which, under the editorship of Francis Jeffrey, had become the scourge of the Tories and the Romantic poets.

Jeffrey had invited Hazlitt to become a reviewer for the *Edinburgh Review* in 1814, the year in which he himself had reviewed Wordsworth's *Excursion* with the notorious and laconic comment, 'This will never do'. Though it became known for the forthright expression of its political opinions, the *Edinburgh Review* soon established a reputation for its literary reviews. While it welcomed change in politics, its literary values were traditional; Jeffrey disliked all modern poetry and looked back to the Elizabethan period as the high-water mark of literary achievement, and next best to this the Augustanism of the eighteenth century. He preferred Crabbe to Coleridge, Rogers to Wordsworth, and Campbell to Southey. His criticism of Byron brought about that splendid retaliatory poem, *English Bards and Scotch Reviewers*, and his review of *Marmion* made Scott swear he would never write for the *Edinburgh* again. Where other men, even other contributors to the *Edinburgh*, judged Jeffrey to be cantankerous and malicious, Hazlitt found in him a patron and benefactor. He paid Hazlitt liberally and even went so far as to write a laudatory review of *Characters of Shakespeare's Plays* in his own periodical. Their good relations were checked for a time by the *Edinburgh*'s cool review of *The Spirit of the Age* in 1825, almost certainly written by Jeffrey himself, in which Hazlitt was advised 'to say sensible things in a plain way' rather than to write for effect and to eschew 'the eternal desire to strike and surprise'. Hazlitt withdrew his services in dudgeon and resumed them only when there was a change of editors, but their friendship was repaired later and it was to Jeffrey that Hazlitt appealed on his deathbed for a loan of £10 to clear his debts. Jeffrey, generous with money as always, promptly sent £50 and allowed Hazlitt to die in peace and dignity.

In 1818–19 Hazlitt gave three courses of lectures, the first of which was attended by Keats who had become a firm friend and admirer, and these were subsequently published as *On the English Poets*, *On the English Comic Writers*, and *On the Dramatic Literature of the Age of Elizabeth*. Though written with the motive of earning money, these were the product of reflection and the wide reading he was able to do when freed from the demands of journalism. Together they form an extended survey of English literature with a concentration on those periods and authors which gave him special pleasure. The lectures provided him with an escape from contemporary disputes into a world of disinterested pleasure. To most of his contemporaries Hazlitt must have appeared a man of bustle and contention, angry and disputatious, concerned only with the rancorous issues of the time. But there was another side to his character; behind this angry polemicist lay a contemplative man who sought relief in an ideal world of artistic delight. Not that he had much time for the 'pure' pleasures of literature, for literature to him was a reflection of life and its values were the values of life as we know it. Nevertheless, the world of books was a kingdom of the mind where he could escape from the distractions of the present. In his lecture 'On Poetry in General' which introduced his *Lectures on the English Poets* he wrote, 'If poetry is a dream, the business of life is much the same. If it is a fiction, made up of what we wish things to be, and fancy that they are, because we wish them so, there is no other nor better reading'. He was not a scholarly critic, for he was impatient of dates and chronology, nor was he a prescriptive critic who judged literature by principles and rules; he was above all a critic who tried to communicate his personal enthusiasm for what he admired. This gave his criticism greater generosity and less rancour than his political writings, but it did not prevent the expression of prejudice, for prejudice is often a kind of personal preference.

Hazlitt had already demonstrated his critical generosity in his comments on Burke in the *Eloquence of the British Senate* in 1807. He admired Burke as a thinker and even more as a writer, though he disagreed profoundly with him on the French Revolution. One of Burke's principles was what Hazlitt described as a natural prejudice. 'He was therefore right in saying that it is no objection to an institution, that it is founded on *prejudice*, but the contrary, if that prejudice is natural and right; that is, if it arises from those circumstances which are properly subjects of feeling and association, not from any defect or perversion of the understanding in those things which fall properly under its jurisdiction. On this profound maxim he took his stand.' In this sense it is natural and right for a man to be prejudiced in favour of his own wife and children, even if they are not superior to those of other men.

Hazlitt shows the same kind of prejudice in his treatment of those authors for whom he has some sympathy. When he is out of sympathy with their opinions he can still write, at least in these *Lectures*, more in sorrow than in anger. Even his remarks on Wordsworth and Coleridge lose some of the acerbity of his earlier comments. So he can say of the one that 'Mr Wordsworth is the most original poet now living ... and the less Mr Wordsworth's general merits have been understood, the more necessary is it to insist upon them', and to pay to the other what amounts to a tribute, even if a sharply qualified one. Writing of Coleridge, he remembers the glory that surrounded him at Shrewsbury.

> He was the first poet I ever knew. His genius at that time had angelic wings, and fed on manna. He talked on for ever; and you wished him to talk on for ever. His thoughts did not seem to come with labour and

> effort; but as if borne on the gusts of genius, and as if the wings of his imagination lifted him from off his feet. His voiced rolled on the ear like the pealing organ, and its sound alone was the music of thought. His mind was clothed with wings; and raised on them he lifted philosophy to heaven. In his descriptions, you then saw the progress of human happiness and liberty in bright and never-ending succession, like the steps of Jacob's ladder, with airy shapes ascending and descending, and with the voice of God at the top of the ladder.

But the earlier glory is used to point the contrast with Coleridge's present state.

> And shall I, who heard him then, listen to him now? Not I! ... that spell is broke; that time is gone for ever; that voice is heard no more: but still the recollection comes rushing by with thought of long-past years, and rings in my ears with never-dying sound.[1]

From 1808 to 1812 the Hazlitts continued to live at Winterslow, though Hazlitt himself made lengthy stays in London. But from then on Hazlitt, his wife, and their small son moved to a house in York Street, Westminster, which had once been the home of Milton and more recently had been occupied by James Mill. His landlord was the philosopher, Jeremy Bentham, with whom his relations were often strained because of failure to pay the rent. Many years later when he had left York Street, he gave an astringent account in *The Spirit of the Age* of Bentham's utilitarian cast of mind; this had connived at a scheme for desecrating the house and garden, which had been 'the cradle of *Paradise Lost*', and permitting a road to be built so that 'the idle rabble of Westminster' could pass across this hallowed ground. Though living in London he sometimes returned to Winterslow and stayed at the Hut, a small inn where he could read and write, undistracted by the cares of business and the demands of journalism. In the Wiltshire countryside he could lie, as he wrote in one of his essays, 'whole mornings on a sunny bank on Salisbury Plain, without any object before me, neither knowing nor caring how time passes, and thus "with light-winged toys of feathered Idleness" to melt down hours to moments'. It was here that he prepared his lectures on the English comic writers and wrote the essays for John Scott's *London Magazine* which afterwards were published in two of his best books, *Table Talk* (1821–2) and *The*

[1] *Lectures on the English Poets*, Lecture VIII, 'On the Living Poets'.

Plain Speaker (1826). Hazlitt needed a retreat not only from professional but domestic troubles, for his marriage went from bad to worse. By 1819 his relations with his wife had reached breaking point. No woman could have tolerated for long the strains he imposed upon Sarah Hazlitt. A few might have borne the financial straits he reduced her to, and others his ill-temper and adultery, but no one would have borne these and accepted as well his flagrant promiscuity and his habit of taking their young son on his visits to the various women of easy virtue he associated with. At the end of the year he and his wife separated and in 1820 Hazlitt took lodgings in Southampton Buildings

It was here that he became infatuated with his landlord's daughter, Sarah Walker. The strange story is chronicled in *Liber Amoris* in which Hazlitt laid bare his heart with astonishing candour. He was now forty-two and Sarah Walker a girl half his age. She was anything but a paragon of beauty or virtue, though probably out of her depth in such an affair, and the tantalizing manner in which she trifled with him inflamed his passion until it assumed the character of an obsession. Hazlitt invested this unremarkable and flirtatious girl with a romantic aura that reflected his own emotional needs and had little objective reality. The rhapsodical flights of *Liber Amoris* read like the yearnings of a young man whose first experience of love expresses itself in a vision of idealized and unattainable perfection. We discern in them the dammed up feelings which had never found satisfaction in his own unhappy marriage.

> Is my love then in the power of fortune, or of her caprice? No, I will have it lasting as it is pure; and I will make a Goddess of her, and build a temple to her in my heart, and worship her on indestructible altars, and raise statues to her: and my homage shall be unblemished as her unrivalled symmetry of form; and when that fails, the memory of it shall survive; and my bosom shall be proof to scorn, as hers has been to pity; and I will pursue her with an unrelenting love, and sue to be her slave, and tend her steps without notice and without reward; and serve her living, and mourn for her when dead.

Alongside these flights of fancy in *Liber Amoris* are passages which reveal a far more earthy and sensual love. This erotic passion was far removed from the purity of his visionary joy, but in Hazlitt's feverish state the two worked together in a gathering frenzy.

By the end of 1821 Hazlitt decided to seek a divorce and,

because this was easier to secure under Scottish law, he devised a plan which took him and his wife to Edinburgh. In February 1822 he stayed for a month at Renton in Berwickshire, where he wrote a series of essays for the *New Monthly Magazine*, later to appear as the second volume of *Table Talk*, and then journeyed to the Scottish capital where his wife joined him in April. While the divorce proceedings were in train Hazlitt paid a brief visit to London to see Sarah Walker, full of foreboding now that she would reject him and that his love had been betrayed. In July the divorce was completed and he and his wife parted on terms which, if not cordial, were at least civilized. She was practical and sensible, as always, and here perhaps was the core of what had always separated them. Hazlitt returned to London at once, but found when he got there that his worst fears had been realized. The effect on him was catastrophic. He could end *Liber Amoris* in a state of sad resignation, 'Her image seems fast "going into the wastes of time", like a weed that the wave bears farther and farther from me ... no flower will ever bloom on earth to glad my heart again!', but before he reached that state he had to pass through a period when his unrequited love alternated with hatred and bitterness. Contemporary accounts all speak of him as insane or demented at this time, of his sending his associates to spy on Sarah, compulsively recounting his misfortune to any who would listen to him, and unable to work or pay his bills. This was a period when in a lifetime of adversities his spirits and his fortunes were at their lowest. The only relief he found was in art and the first writing he managed to accomplish after his rejection were essays on the galleries he visited. He contributed these essays on the Dulwich Gallery, the pictures at Windsor Castle, the pictures at Hampton Court, and others to the *London* and they appeared later as *Sketches of the Principle Picture-Galleries in England*. We should not blame Sarah Walker unduly for the misery she caused Hazlitt, for she had been caught up in events which she did not understand and by a personality more complex than she could comprehend. Nor, perhaps, should we censure Hazlitt, for he was swept away by emotions which should have been liberated much earlier in life. Even *Liber Amoris* which appeared in 1823 and which so excited his enemies and fed their malicious prurience, should be seen as a kind of abreaction and though its authorship was known at once, we should remember that it was published anonymously.

Hazlitt spent a good deal of this period at the Hut, at

Winterslow. His recovery was slow, but as the emotional forces which had been released in his personality became integrated, his work achieved a new power. At the end of 1821 he was asked to write for the *Liberal*, a new periodical launched by Byron, Shelley, and Leigh Hunt. The invitation was surprising, for in spite of their shared political opinions, Hazlitt did not admire Shelley as a poet and his relations with Byron were less than cordial following his adverse reviews of Byron's poetry. But his association with them was short-lived. The *Liberal* was dogged with misfortune from the beginning. Shelley was drowned in July 1822, John Hunt was charged with libelling George III for printing Byron's 'The Vision of Judgment' which appeared in the first number, and Leigh Hunt quarrelled with Byron. The fourth number was its last, but during its brief lifetime, which provoked a storm of abuse, Hazlitt wrote for it some of his best essays. In its third number appeared 'My First Acquaintance with Poets' and for the second he contributed 'On the Scotch Character' and 'On the Spirit of Monarchy', all of which are written with a wonderful command of language and the first of which is one of his masterpieces. To the same year belongs his *Characteristics: in the Manner of Rochefoucault's Maxims*, published anonymously in 1823, and made up of material he had intended for the *Liberal*. These worldly-wise observations on man and society reflect the cynicism and weariness which still clouded Hazlitt's mind. From the smartness of 'Vice is man's nature: virtue is a habit – or a mask', of 'There is often a good deal of spleen at the bottom of benevolence', it is a short step to the bruised sensibility which shows in 'We grow tired of ourselves, much more of other people', and 'An accomplished coquet excites the passions of others, in proportion as she feels none herself'.

For evidence of a full recovery of spirits we have to turn to *The Spirit of the Age*, though Hazlitt told Landor that he had written it in a 'depression of body and mind'. This is his greatest book and it shows a renewed and, indeed, a greater mental energy than anything he had written before. A couple of the essays he included in it came from his earlier periodical publications, but the great bulk of it was new. The work began in Winterslow late in 1823 when he wrote a short biographical study of his old landlord, Jeremy Bentham, which appeared in the *New Monthly* the next spring. This was followed by four sketches of eminent contemporaries for the same periodical, which together with one on Canning written for the *Examiner*, he gathered together with seventeen new essays to form his book. *The Spirit of the Age* is more than a collection of separate biographies, it has a structure and coherence which give the work a cumulative effect and provide a synoptic view of the period. It can be seen as his *Biographia Literaria*, though it deals only with his contemporaries and not with earlier figures who had influenced him, and as his considered judgement on his own generation. He discusses, of course, not only those who have influenced him positively, but those with whom he disagrees, and most frequently those who manage to fall into both these categories. He sees his own age animated by a great debate carried on by those who are traditionalists, some of them, indeed, reactionaries, and those who believe in reform and experiment. From his vantage point in middle life, he observes these opposing forces and considers that great opportunities have been lost, that his own period has been one of unfulfilled hopes and broken promises. He does not lack sympathy with tradition, but regards it as something which must be vitalized and carried forward by the talents of individuals in every generation. The tragedy of his own age is that though there have been men of great talents, some of them, indeed, geniuses, they have failed to do this. There is thus a certain sadness in his view of men and events, but never despair. He lives in hope that the failures of today may become the achievements of tomorrow.

The temper of Hazlitt's writing in *The Spirit of the Age* is more balanced and less strident than in much of his previous work. He can still express vehement dislike on occasion and his sarcasm can be biting, as when he says of Gifford that he is admirably qualified to be editor of the *Quarterly Review* since he is fitted to this situation 'by a happy combination of defects, natural and acquired'. It would be asking too much of Hazlitt to write dispassionately of one who had attacked him personally throughout the years, but generally his tone is generous in its understanding of human motives and behaviour, and ready to balance virtues against faults. In *Liber Amoris* he had preached what he called the religion of love, a strange compound of *eros* and *agape*, but here he is moved by a religion of humanity. He realizes that any improvement in the condition of man must reconcile the claims of both the heart and the head, that plans for social reform must be made not only by the light of the intellect but with regard for the emotions. Many schemes for improvement are too narrow in their view of human nature. So he criticizes Bentham for basing everything on the principle of utility: 'He has a great contempt for out-of-door prospects, for green fields and trees, and is referring every thing to Utility. There is a little narrowness in this; for if all the sources of satisfaction are taken away, what is to become of utility itself? It is, indeed, the great fault of this able and extraordinary man, that he has concentrated his faculties and feelings too entirely on one subject and pursuit and has not "looked enough abroad into universality".' Similarly, he attacks Malthus not for the strict theoretical side of the argument concerning population, but for his failure to acknowledge that men are free to arrange things for the good of all. The growth of population should be checked not by vice and misery, but by moral restraint, and the poor should not be treated as the victims of natural forces. His denunciation of Wilberforce rests upon the charge that Wilberforce concentrated upon the abolition of slavery abroad, but failed to expose evil at home. This myopic view was a fault not only of the intellect, but of moral sensibility, and led Wilberforce into hypocrisy.

> His patriotism, his philanthropy are not so ill-bred, as to quarrel with his loyalty or to banish him from the first circles. He preaches vital Christianity to untutored savages, and tolerates its worst abuses in civilized states ... There is in all this an appearance of a good deal of cant and tricking. His patriotism may be accused of being servile, his humanity ostentatious, his loyalty conditional, his religion a mixture of fashion and fanaticism.

One of the best portraits in *The Spirit of the Age* for understanding Hazlitt's analysis of the contemporary situation is that of Sir Walter Scott, for Scott's interpretation of history was very different from his own. Hazlitt had every reason for disliking Scott, whom he regarded as a reactionary Tory and time-server, and his admiration for Scott's novels came to him late. This was the paradox he had to face: how a man whose political views were so antipathetic to him could write novels 'whose worst is better than any other person's best'. What he admired so much was Scott's ability to take the reader into a story that captured his imagination, that ranged over the whole of life, from the highest to the lowest, and that showed sympathy and understanding for the human condition. 'What a power is that of genius!', he exclaims, 'What a world of thought and feeling is thus rescued from oblivion! How many hours of heartfelt satisfaction has our author given to the gay and thoughtless! How many sad hearts has he soothed in pain and solitude!' Scott's great gift is to be able to give the universal concrete expression; it is the gift of the imagination and especially of the historical imagination, which can represent life as it really was. But Scott has fatal limitations and defects; his mind is timid, it 'does not project itself beyond this into the world unknown, but mechanically shrinks back as from the edge of a precipice'. Scott seeks refuge from the present in history: 'Sir Walter would make a bad hand of a description of the Millennium, unless he could lay the scene in Scotland five hundred years ago'. He is a writer 'who, from the height of his genius looking abroad into nature, and scanning the recesses of the human heart, "winked and shut his apprehension up" to every thought on purpose that tended to the future good of mankind'.

It is a measure of Hazlitt's sympathetic understanding that his most eloquent tributes are paid to those with whom he disagreed most profoundly: Scott, Burke (who lies outside the purview of *The Spirit of the Age*), Wordsworth, and Coleridge. He comes once again in these portraits to a considered judgement of the last two, whose influence, through friendship and alienation, remained with him always. He regards Wordsworth as the archetypal figure of the period. 'Mr Wordsworth's genius is a pure emanation of the Spirit of the Age.' His earlier poetry reflects the stirring of revolutionary change with which the age began. 'It is one of the innovations of the time. It partakes of, and is carried along with, the revolutionary movement of our age: the political changes of the day were the model on which he formed and conducted his political experiments.' Since then Wordsworth has withdrawn to a life of contemplation. Hazlitt gives him credit for resisting the beguilement of material ambitions and worldly fame, but regrets that he has retreated from the challenges of the times and 'passed his life in solitary musing or in daily converse with the face of nature'. Wordsworth's later poetry now reflects this concern with the self and is no more than an association of images in the poet's own mind. 'He has dwelt among pastoral scenes, till each object has become connected with a thousand feelings, a link in the chain of thought, a fibre of his own heart.' Hazlitt sees him rescued by a growing popular esteem from the sad fate that might otherwise have awaited him – 'that of becoming the God of his own idolatry'.

There, then, are two tendencies of the age; to retreat into history or to withdraw into the recesses of one's own mind. Another is to engage in endless talk as an escape from action. 'The present is an age of talkers, and not of doers; and the reason is that the world is growing old.' Nothing exemplifies this more clearly for Hazlitt than what he considered the wasted genius of Coleridge, whose voice, as he recalls it, 'is like the echo of the congregated roar of the "dark rearward and abyss" of thought'. Hazlitt gives a brilliant sketch of Coleridge's intellectual and spiritual pilgrimage, tracing his progress from the time when he had been a revolutionary and a democrat, when he 'had kindled his affections at the blaze of the French Revolution, and sang for joy, when the towers of the Bastille and the proud places of the insolent and the oppressor fell', through a discipleship of Godwin and Hartley, and allegiance to the Platonists, mystics, and 'Bishop Berkeley's fairy-world', until he 'lost himself in the labyrinths ... of the Kantean philosophy, and amongst the cabalistic names of Fichte and Schelling, and God knows who'. It is a sorry story of dissipated powers, says Hazlitt, 'Alas! "Frailty, thy name is *Genius*!" ... such and so little is the mind of man'. Coleridge had given excuses by his 'casuistry and a musical voice' for those who dared not risk unpopularity or who sought state favours, but while they entered the citadels of privilege and public acclaim, he himself remained outside, 'pitching his tent upon the barren waste without, and having no abiding place nor city of refuge!' He had achieved neither position nor place, nor would he win lasting fame. It is a sad valedictory to one whom Hazlitt had once worshipped.

It would be an error, of course, to mistake Hazlitt's mellowness for objectivity and his pronouncements often derive from a pattern of preconceived ideas which he imposes on his age. His insistence that Scott seeks to escape from the present into the refuge of the past does scant justice to Scott's belief that we can see an image of ourselves in the mirror of history and that history is the best discipline we can have for tackling present problems. He fails to see this, of course, because he has no sympathy with Scott's Tory philosophy. Equally he ignores Wordsworth's concern for 'Joy in widest commonalty spread', which accompanied his 'bliss in solitude'. Worst of all is what amounts to his patronage of Coleridge, who merited his pity even less than his anger. Though he admires Coleridge's erudition, he fails to see the significance of his philosophical speculation and does not recognize, as Mill did a few years later, that Coleridge was one of the great seminal minds of the period. These are all limitations which spring from his deeply held convictions; they may be mistaken and must detract from any claim he had to be a profound thinker, but at least they are free of malice.

While Hazlitt was completing *The Spirit of the Age* he embarked upon marriage for the second time. We do not know the time or the date of the marriage, though it was probably in April 1824 in Edinburgh, and very little about his new wife. Some said that Mrs Isabella Bridgewater was the widow of an army colonel, others the widow of a barrister, but all agreed that she was a woman of character and that Hazlitt was lucky to have married her. By August of that year the couple left on a Continental tour, staying in Paris for three months, when Hazlitt visited the Louvre once again, and proceeding in January, 1825, to Italy. Hazlitt recounted their journey in *Notes of a Journey through France and Italy,* published in that year. After a few weeks in Switzerland they returned to England in the autumn.

In 1826 Hazlitt gathered together the essays which were published as *The Plain Speaker* and began writing as articles his 'conversations' with the painter, James Northcote, an old friend of thirty years' standing. In the summer he went to France where he stayed for fourteen months working on what he considered his *magnum opus,* the *Life of Napoleon,* and contributing a string of articles for the periodicals at home. He returned in October 1827, but his wife did not accompany him and, as far as we know, they never met again. Some said that Hazlitt's son was unhappy with his step-mother and that this brought about a split, but Hazlitt himself has left us no account of their separation. His main concern on returning to England was the publication of his *Life of Napoleon.* The first two volumes appeared in January 1828, but Hazlitt's high hopes for what he regarded as the crowning achievement of his career were speedily dashed, for the reception they were given was decidedly cool. Undeterred by the bankruptcy of his publishers which brought about his own arrest for debt, he set about preparing for publication the third and fourth volumes. These appeared in the year of his death and he probably did not see them in print. This was just as well, for his attempt to defend the beliefs of a lifetime, the cause of the French Revolution and Napoleon as the embodiment of the aspirations that were then given birth, his attack on the Tories for refusing to see the need for reform, and his lamentation for Napoleon's final defeat, all met with a stony silence. Even if one were able to share his exaggerated and partisan views, one would still have to confess that Hazlitt's work is prolix and tedious. Even Lamb, generous to the last in trying to see something to admire in the writings of his friend, had to admit that he skipped parts of it.

On returning from France, Hazlitt retired again to Winterslow. The failure of his publishers obliged him to continue with his journalism, although in 1828 he had written one of his finest pieces, 'A Farewell to Essay-Writing', which first appeared in the *London Weekly Review*. Though embroiled to the end in dispute and dissension, he seemed now to be more withdrawn into his own memories. His emotions are recollected and expressed in tranquillity. 'Food, warmth, sleep, and a book; these are all I at present ask', he writes at the beginning of his 'Farewell'. '... give me the robin redbreast, pecking the crumbs at the door, or warbling on the leafless spray, the same glancing form that has followed me wherever I have been ... or the rich notes of the thrush that startle the ear of winter ... To these I adhere, and am faithful, for they are true to me'. Though few now shared his most cherished political convictions and though events seemed to have conspired against him, he remains true to his youthful vision. 'One great ground of confidence and support has, indeed, been struck from under my feet; but I have made it up to myself by proportionable pertinacity of opinion. The success of the great cause, to which I had vowed myself, was to me more than all the world ... But my conviction of the right was only established by the triumph of the wrong; and my earliest hopes will be my last regrets.' He recalls earlier and happier years at Winterslow, when Charles and Mary Lamb had visited him. 'I used to walk out at this time with Mr and Miss Lamb of an evening, to look at the Claude Lorraine skies over our heads melting from azure into purple and gold, and to gather mushrooms, that sprang up at our feet, to throw into our hashed mutton at supper.' This association of ideas leads him to the pleasures afforded by art and reminds him of his visits to picture-galleries. It is these memories which give him strength to face what lies ahead.

> It is in looking back to such scenes that I draw my best consolation for the future. Later impressions come and go, and serve to fill up the intervals; but these are my standing resource, my true classics. If I have had few real pleasures or advantages, my ideas, from their sinewy texture, have been to me in the nature of realities; and if I should not be able to add to the stock, I can live by husbanding the interest.

Not that he had much future to look forward to. Back in London he worked as drama critic of the *Examiner* and found pleasure again in his old love of the theatre. But his health began to deteriorate; worn out by constant industry, personal and professional disappointment, by poverty, and by calumny, he seemed prematurely old. Finally he suffered from cancer of the stomach. He died, aged fifty-two, on 18 September 1830 and was buried in St Anne's churchyard in Soho. His life had been marked by hardship and misery, and yet his last words, according to his son were, 'Well, I have had a happy life'. He was sustained at the last, as he had always been in adversity, by memories of his childhood and youth, when the world lay bright before him. Always in times of misery he had found consolation in memories of the innocence of childhood (something that links him to Blake and Wordsworth), and new hope in a vision of what life might be. Once in his essay on 'The Dulwich Gallery' he had written of himself as a boy. 'See him there, the urchin, seated in the sun, with a book in his hand, and the wall at his back. He has a thicker wall before him – the wall that parts him from the future ... he thinks that he will one day write a book, and have his name repeated by thousands of readers ... Come hither, thou poor little fellow, and let us change places with thee if you wilt'. The urchin's wish had been granted; he had had to 'feed poor, and lie hard, and be contented and happy, and think what a fine thing it is to be an author, and dream of immortality'. Nor would Hazlitt on his deathbed have had it otherwise.

Hazlitt's achievement as a man of letters lies in his essays and his literary criticism. As an essayist he belongs to that English tradition of writing which runs through Bacon, Addison, Steele, Johnson, and Hume, but he also owes something to the French writers Montaigne and Rousseau, whose work was more confessional and personal. Writing for him was concerned not with lifeless abstractions but was the embodiment of a man's attitude to life, his values and passions as well as his intellect. That is why he could say in the 'Character of Mr Burke', 'The only specimen of Burke is, *all that he wrote*'. Nevertheless, while there is this personal reference in nearly all he wrote, he was a keen observer and critic of human affairs and of his fellow men. The essay was for him the form above all others most suited to bringing together the mind of the author and the pageant of human experience. The essayist's art consists, he writes in 'On the Periodical Essayists', 'in applying the talents and resources of the mind to all that mixed mass of human affairs, which, though not included under the head of any regular art, science, or profession, falls under the cognizance of the writer and "comes home to the business and bosoms of men" ... it makes familiar with the world of men and women, records their actions, assigns their motives, exhibits their whims, characterizes their pursuits in all their singular and endless variety, ridicules their absurdities, exposes their inconsistencies'. He goes on to elaborate the notion that the essay is ideally fitted to approach life with a method that is concrete and particular rather than *a priori* and theoretical. 'It is in morals and manners what the experimental is in natural philosophy, as opposed to the dogmatical method. It does not deal in sweeping clauses of proscription and anathema, but in nice distinctions and liberal constructions. It makes up its general accounts from details, its few theories from many facts.'

One might find it difficult at first glance to apply this to his own practice as an essayist, for Hazlitt always seems prone to view things through the spectacles of his own preconceptions, to confuse politics and poetry, to see men as actors in a great historical drama which he has largely written himself. There are few of his essays which do not include at least a passing reference to his revolutionary convictions, and in many his radical opinions throw a shadow across the page. At times, indeed, this tendency becomes tedious, but what redeems him is that his polemicism is mitigated by common sense and honesty. In his essay 'On Personal Character', for instance, he observes that human character is much more intransigent than reformers would like to admit, that to change men's circumstances does not always lead to an improvement of behaviour, that different nations have their own national characteristics which remain pretty constant, that genetic inheritance is more powerful than the habits we acquire by education and social convention.

> We may refine, we may disguise, we may equivocate, we may compound for our vices, without getting rid of them; as we change our liquors, but do not leave off drinking. We may, in this respect, look forward to a decent and moderate, rather than a thorough and radical reform ... we may improve the mechanism, if not the texture of society; that is, we may improve the physical circumstances of individuals and their general relations to the State, though the internal character, like the grain in wood, or the sap in trees, that still rises, bend them how you will, may remain nearly the same.

Hazlitt was least doctrinaire when it came to human nature.

This understanding of, and sympathy for, human nature in all its complexity can be seen in his essays which deal with the novel and the theatre. Scott's works, he wrote, 'are almost like a new edition of human nature. This is indeed to be an author!' In his lecture 'On the English Novelists' he says that fiction is a representation of life; what we learn from it is what we learn from life itself, not theoretical knowledge but knowledge given us by direct acquaintance. 'We find there a close imitation of men and manners; we see the very web and texture of society as it really exists, and as we meet with it when we come into the world.' Similarly the theatre teaches us not by precept but by extending and enriching our sensibilities; it holds up a mirror in which we see our faults and brings before us a vision of what we might be. The players, he writes in 'On Actors and Acting',

> shew us all that we are, all that we wish to be, and all that we dread to be. The stage is an epitome, a bettered likeness of the world, with the dull part left out... What brings the resemblance nearer is, that, as *they* imitate us, we, in our turn imitate them ... They teach us when to laugh and when to weep, when to hate, upon principle and with a good grace! Wherever there is a playhouse, the world will not go on amiss. The stage not only refines the manners, but it is the best teacher of morals, for it is the truest and most intelligent picture of life.

Even further removed from polemics was Hazlitt's love of painting. Here was an activity which had no other end than itself. 'You sit down to your task, and are happy,' he wrote in 'On the Pleasure of Painting',

> No angry passions rise to disturb the silent progress of the work, to

> shake the hand, or dim the brow; no irritable humours are set afloat: you have no absurd opinions to combat, no point to strain, no adversary to crush, no fool to annoy – you are actuated by fear or favour to no man. There is 'no juggling here', no sophistry, no intrigue, no tampering with the evidence ... but you resign yourself into the hands of a greater power, that of Nature, with the simplicity of a child, and the devotion of an enthusiast.

Painting not only provided an escape but sharpened his powers of observation so that he could hit off a man's appearance or manner by the use of significant detail. Some of his essays demonstrate this ability of the portrait painter to depict character in visual description, as when he writes, perhaps unfairly, of Coleridge's habit of 'shifting from one side of the foot-path to the other', and uses it as evidence of the poet's instability of purpose, or describes Wordsworth as 'grave, saturnine, with a slight indication of sly humour, kept under by the manners of the age or by the pretensions of the person. He has a peculiar sweetness in his smile, and great depth and manliness and a rugged harmony in the tones of his voice. His manner of reading his own poetry is particularly imposing'.

At bottom Hazlitt was a solitary, shy in company, ill at ease unless with a few intimate friends, and even then often gauche and silent. He found refreshment of spirit most at Winterslow, where alone with Nature he could walk in the winter or lie upon a sunny bank in summer, where he could survey the landscape, delight in animal life, and feel himself part of the progress of the seasons. It was at Winterslow that he wrote his essay 'On Living to One's-Self' where he explains, 'what I mean by living to one's-self is living in the world, as in it, not of it: it is as if no one knew there was such a person, and you wished no one to know it: it is to be a silent spectator of the mighty scene of things, not an object of attention or curiosity in it; to take a thoughtful, anxious interest in what is passing in the world, but not to feel the slightest inclination to make or meddle with it ... this sort of dreaming existence is the best'. Those who see Hazlitt only as a partisan fail to take account of this more important side of him. Without this dreaming, contemplative, solitary nature, drawing upon a store of memories and associations, reflecting upon his own life and the experience of others, he would not have been the great writer he was.

Great writing depends also, of course, upon style, upon the

ability to use language to express one's thoughts and feelings exactly and movingly. One of the best-known criticisms of Hazlitt's style is De Quincey's, though it relates to Hazlitt as a lecturer and not a writer. In an essay on Charles Lamb which he contributed to the *North British Review* for November 1848, De Quincey declared, 'No man can be eloquent whose thoughts are abrupt, insulated, capricious, and (to borrow an impressive word from Coleridge) non-sequacious. Eloquence resides not in separate or fractional ideas, but in the relations of manifold ideas, and in the mode of their evolution from each other ... Now Hazlitt's brilliancy is seen chiefly in separate splinterings of phrase or image ... A flash, a solitary flash, and all is gone'. It is a damaging charge, but Hazlitt had said as much as this himself when he described his essay-writing in 'On the Pleasure of Painting'. 'I seldom see my way a page or even a sentence beforehand', he wrote, 'and when I have as by a miracle escaped, I trouble myself little more about them. I sometimes have to write them twice over ... For a person to read his own works over with any great delight, he ought first to forget that he ever wrote them ... I have more satisfaction in my own thoughts than in dictating them to others.'

This is a strength as well as weakness in Hazlitt's composition, for his style has spontaneity and freshness; it gives one the pleasure of good conversation and we feel as we read his work that we are getting to know an interesting acquaintance and entering his mind and personality. This is very much Hazlitt's intention, for in his essay 'On Familiar Style', he tells us that 'To write a genuine familiar or truly English style, is to write as any one would speak in common conversation, who had a thorough command and choice of words, or who could discourse with ease, force, and perspicuity, setting aside all pedantic and oratorical flourishes'. Though spontaneous his style draws upon a wide range of reading, ever ready at his call, either by direct and apt quotation or by allusion. His cadences often echo Shakespeare, whose plays he knew intimately, and the Authorized Version of the Bible, which he must have heard Sunday by Sunday at his father's chapel in Wem, but there are also an elegance, an exactness, and a pithiness of expression which come from his reading of the great prose stylists of the eighteenth century: Burke, whom he admired above all as a writer, the essayists such as Addison and Steele (though not Johnson whose orotundity seemed to him oppressive), and the philosophers, especially David Hume, whom he thought Coleridge had dismissed too lightly.

We should not forget that Hazlitt regarded himself as a philosopher and that he had roots in the empiricist tradition of the eighteenth century. His first book, written after years of study, was *An Essay on the Principles of Human Action* and this was followed not very long after by his *Lectures on Philosophy*. Hazlitt is generally considered an impressionistic and not a philosophical critic, but behind his critical judgements are certain assumptions and principles, including an implicit theory of the mind, and these derive in the main from empiricism. This philosophy is often confused with rationalism, but empiricism believed that our knowledge is derived from experience and while it tried to bring as great an area of human experience as possible within the bounds of rational explanation, it was often profoundly sceptical of the powers of reason. At its most sceptical it could declare with Hobbes that 'the thoughts are to the desires, as scouts, and spies, to range abroad, and find the way to the things desired' (*Leviathan*, I, viii), or with Hume that 'Reason is, and ought only to be, the slave of the passions' (*A Treatise of Human Nature*, II, iii). This kind of scepticism chimes in well with Hazlitt's distrust of any attempt to explain men entirely in terms of reason and throws a clear light on his approach to literature.

Literature for Hazlitt is a matter of the emotions. He is impatient with neo-classical rules and categories; 'Poetry', he writes in 'On Poetry in General', 'is the language of the imagination and the passions.' It is not always easy to decide what he meant by 'imagination'. Though he was scornful of the new German philosophy which encouraged Coleridge to elaborate his famous distinction between the fancy and the imagination, in many places he adopts language reminiscent of Coleridge's. There is little to show, however, that he grasped the complexity of Coleridge's theory. He quotes with approval (though inaccurately) Bacon's famous dictum that poetry 'has something divine in it, because it raises the mind and hurries it into sublimity, by conforming the shows of things to the desires of the soul, instead of subjecting the soul to external things, as reason and theory do', but what gives it this character, according to Hazlitt, is the force of passion and the desire to gratify our own wishes. He does not regard the imagination as, in Coleridge's phrase, 'the agent of the reason', and the knowledge it gives comes not from an interplay between symbol and concept, but from our direct perception of the created world the poet presents, a world like the one we know but shaped and given life by the poet's 'gusto', a term much favoured by Hazlitt. The romantic notion that poetry seeks to embody an idea in the poet's mind has to find a place in his thought alongside the Aristotelian view that poetry is a representation of life as it is or ought to be. When he turns from poetry to the novel – and he was the first critic to take the novel seriously – it is the Aristotelian view which predominates.

Hazlitt's psychology is the eighteenth-century associationist one, but because he does not care for a mechanical interpretation of this doctrine he shares Wordsworth's belief that our ideas are associated under the influence of emotion rather than simply by contiguity of space and time, and that poetry, to use the phraseology of the Preface to *Lyrical Ballads*, is concerned with 'the manner in which we associate ideas in a state of excitement' and is 'the spontaneous overflow of powerful feelings'. Equally our critical judgements are made not by reason, nor the application of rules, but by what we would call emotional sensibility and what the eighteenth century called passion, which for Hazlitt included an imaginative sympathy.

This quality of sympathetic understanding has a central place amid the various critical ideas which Hazlitt holds in suspension and enriches his appreciation of literature. Indeed, it characterizes all he wrote. Although he was, above all, a personal writer, he could by an exercise of the imagination, enter into the lives of men very different from himself. It is true that he was a good hater, but as he remarked in his essay on the subject, hatred is common to us all. 'I have quarrelled with almost all my old friends (they might say this is owing to my bad temper), but they have also quarrelled with one another.' Hatred, then, is not something which separates him from his fellows, but something which unites him to them. 'Life', he says, 'would turn to a stagnant pool, were it not ruffled by the jarring interests, the unruly passions, of men.' The 'passions of men', whether unruly or not, his own as well as those of others, are what concern him. This is why he will always have readers to admire and find pleasure in his work.

Select Bibliography

Listed chronologically, by date of first publication, unless stated otherwise.

BIBLIOGRAPHY

Bibliography of William Hazlitt, by Sir Geoffrey Keynes (1931); second edition revised by G. L. Keynes (Godalming, 1981).
English Romantic Poets and Essayists: A Review of Research and Criticism, ed. C. W. and L. H. Houtchens (New York, 1957; rev. edn. 1966). Contains chapter on Hazlitt by E. W. Schneider.
William Hazlitt: A Reference Guide, by James A. Houck (London, 1977).

EDITIONS OF WORKS BY WILLIAM HAZLITT

Collected Works

The Collected Works, ed. A. R. Walker and A. Glover, with an introduction by W. E. Henley, 12 vols. (London, 1902–6).
The Complete Works, ed P. P. Howe, 21 vols. (London 1930–4). A revision of the Walker and Glover edition, with additional notes, 'The Life of Napoleon', and other uncollected material.

Selections

Hazlitt: Essayist and Critic, ed. A. Ireland (London & New York, 1889).
Essays on Poetry, ed. D. Nichol Smith (London, 1901).
Essays, ed. C. Whibley (London, 1906).
Selections, ed. W. D. Howe (Boston, Mass.,1913).
Hazlitt on English Literature, ed. J. Zeitlin (New York, 1913).
Selected Essays, ed. G. Sampson (Cambridge, 1917).
The Best of Hazlitt, ed. P. P. Howe (London, 1923).

Selected Essays, ed. G. L. Keynes (London: Nonesuch Library, 1930; new edn. 1970.) The best comprehensive selection.
Selections from Lamb and Hazlitt, ed. R.,W. Jepson (London, 1940).
Selected Essays, ed. R. Wilson (London & Edinburgh, 1942).
Hazlitt Painted by Himself, ed. C. M. Maclean (London, 1948).
Liber Amoris and Dramatic Criticisms, ed. C. Morgan (London, 1948).
The Essays: A Selection, ed. C. M. Maclean (London, 1949).
Essays, ed. R. Vallance and J. Hampden (London, 1964).
Selected Writings: William Hazlitt, edited with an introduction by Ronald Blythe (Harmondsworth: Penguin, 1970; rev. edn. 1985).
Selected Writings: William Hazlitt, edited with an introduction by Jon Cook (Oxford, 1991).

Separate Works

An Essay on the Principles of Human Action (London, 1805; 1835 edn. repr. Bristol, 1990). Published anonymously.
Free Thoughts on Public Affairs: or Advice to a Patriot (London, 1806). Published anonymously.
An Abridgement of the Light of Nature Pursued, by Abraham Tucker (London, 1807). Published anonymously.
The Eloquence of the British Senate; or Select Specimens from the Speeches of the most distinguished Parliamentary Speakers, from the beginning of the Reign of Charles I, 2 vols. (London, 1807). Published anonymously.
A Reply to the Essay on Population, by the Rev. T. R. Malthus. In a Series of Letters (London, 1807; repr. New York, 1967). Published anonymously.
A New and Improved Grammar of the English Tongue: For the Use of Schools (London, 1810).
Memoirs of the Late Thomas Holcroft, Written by himself [Hazlitt] *and continued to the time of his death*, 3 vols. (London, 1816); ed. E. Colby, 2 vols. (London, 1925); repr. World's Classics, Oxford, 1926).
The Round Table: A Collection of Essays on Literature, Men and Manners, 2 vols. (Edinburgh, 1817; repr. Oxford, 1991). Reprinted in Everyman's Library, together with *Characters of Shakespeare's Plays*, introduction by Catherine McDonald McClean (London, 1957).
Characters of Shakespeare's Plays (London, 1817; repr. Everyman's Library, London, 1906, and World's Classics, Oxford, 1917).
A View of the English Stage: or, A Series of Dramatic Criticisms (London, 1818); ed. W. Hazlitt Jnr. (London, 1851); ed. W. S. Jackson (London, 1906).
Lectures on the English Poets (London, 1818; repr. in Everyman's Library, London, 1910 and 1955, and World's Classics, Oxford, 1924); ed. F. W. Baxter (Oxford, 1929).
A Letter to William Gifford, Esq. (London, 1819).
Lectures on the English Comic Writers (London, 1819); ed. W. C. Hazlitt

(London, 1869) repr. in World's Classics, Oxford, 1907); ed. A. Johnson, Everyman's Library (London, 1965).

Political Essays, with Sketches of Public Characters (London, 1819); repr. Oxford, 1990).

Lectures Chiefly on the Dramatic Literature of the Age of Elizabeth (London, 1820).

Table Talk, 2 vols. (London, 1821–2); repr. World's Classics Oxford, 1901, and Everyman's Library, London, 1908).

Liber Amoris: or, The New Pygmalion (London, 1823). Published anonymously; ed. R. Le Gallienne (and W. C. Hazlitt) and printed privately, with additional material (London, 1894); ed. C. Morgan (1948); edited with an introduction and notes by Gerald Lahey (New York, 1980); 1893 edition reprinted, with a new introduction by Michael Neve (London, 1985).

Characteristics: in the Manner of Rochefoucault's Maxims (London, 1823). Published anonymously; ed. R. H. Horne (London, 1837; repr. 1927).

Sketches on the Principal Picture Galleries in England (London, 1824).

Select British Poets, or New Elegant Extracts from Chaucer to the Present Time, with Critical Remarks (London, 1824). Withdrawn owing to infringement of copyright in the contemporary section. Published as *Select Poets of Great Britain* (London, 1825), without copyright material.

The Spirit of the Age, or Contemporary Portraits (London, 1825); repr. World's Classics, Oxford, 1904); ed. E. D. Mackerness (London, 1969; Plymouth, 1991).

The Plain Speaker: Opinions on Books, Men and Things, 2 vols. (London, 1826; repr. Everyman's Library, London 1928).

Notes of a Journey through France and Italy (London, 1826).

The Life of Napoleon Bonaparte, 4 vols. (London, 1826–30).

Conversations of James Northcote, Esq., R.A. (London, 1830); ed. E. Gosse (London, 1894); ed. F. Swinnerton (London, 1949).

Literary Remains of the Late William Hazlitt, With a Notice of his Life, by his Son (London, 1836). Twenty-two essays, mainly printed from periodicals.

Painting [by R. B.. Haydon] *and the Fine Arts* [by Hazlitt] (Edinburgh, 1838).

Sketches and Essays, Now First Collected by his Son (London, 1839; repr. in World's Classics, Oxford, 1902). Eighteen essays reprinted from periodicals.

Criticisms on Art: and Sketches of the Picture Galleries of England, ed. W. Hazlitt Jnr., 2 series (1834–44); ed. W. C. Hazlitt as *Essays on the Fine Arts* (London, 1873).

Winterslow: Essays and Characters Written There, ed. W. Hazlitt Jnr. (London, 1850; repr. World's Classics, Oxford 1902).

Men and Manners: Sketches and Essays (London, 1852); facsimile of 1st London edn. repr. 1970).

Memoirs of William Hazlitt, with Portions of his Correspondence, ed. W. C. Hazlitt, 2 vols. (London, 1867).

Lamb and Hazlitt: Further Letters and Records, ed. W. C. Hazlitt (London, 1900).

New Writings of William Hazlitt, ed. P. P. Howe, 2 series (London, 1925–7). Articles reprinted from periodicals and Oxberry's *New English Drama* (London 1818–19).

Hazlitt in the Workshop: The MS of 'The Fight', ed. S. C. Wilcox (Baltimore, Md, 1943).

BIOGRAPHICAL AND CRITICAL STUDIES
(listed alphabetically, by author)

Albrecht, William P., *Hazlitt and the Malthusian Controversy* (Albuquerque, NM, 1950; repr. 1969).

Albrecht, William P., *Hazlitt and the Creative Imagination* (Lawrence, Kans., 1965).

Archer, William, and Robert Lowe (eds.), *Hazlitt on Theatre*, with an introduction by William Archer (New York, 1958).

Baker, Herschel, *William Hazlitt* (Cambridge, Mass., 1962). A major and excellent study of Hazlitt's life, ideas and background.

Barrell, John, *The Political Theory of Painting from Reynolds to Hazlitt: The Body of the Public* (New Haven, Conn., 1986).

Bate, Jonathan, *Shakespearean Constitutions* (Oxford, 1989).

Bate, Walter J., *Criticism: The Major Texts* (New York, 1952).

Bates, H., *William Hazlitt* (London, 1962).

Birrell, A., *William Hazlitt* (London, 1902).

Bloom, Harold (ed.) *William Hazlitt*, with an introduction by Harold Bloom (New York, 1986).

Bromwich, David, *Hazlitt: The Mind of a Critic*, (Oxford, 1984).

Cafarelli, Annette Wheeler, *Prose in the Age of Poets: Romanticism and Biographical Narrative from Johnson to De Quincey* (Philadelphia, Pa., 1990).

Garrod, H. W., *The Profession of Poetry* (Oxford, 1929). Reprints an essay, 'The Place of Hazlitt in English Criticism'.

Hazlitt, W. C., *Four Generations of a Literary Family*, 2 vols. (London, 1897).

Heller, Janet Ruth, *Coleridge, Lamb, Hazlitt and the Reader of Drama* (Columbia, Mo., 1990).

Howe, P. P., *The Life of William Hazlitt* (London, 1922); revised 1928 and 1947 (Harmondsworth, 1949). Now superseded by Herschel Baker's study.

Jack, Ian, *English Literature 1815–32* (Oxford, 1963). Chapter 9, 'Hazlitt';

contains a very useful bibliography.
Jones, Stanley, *Hazlitt, a Life: From Winterslow to Frith Street* (Oxford, 1989; repr. 1991).
Ker, William, P., *Collected Essays*, vol. 1 (London, 1925). Includes an essay on Hazlitt.
Kinnaird, John, *William Hazlitt: A Critic of Power* (New York, 1978).
Maclean, C. M., *Born under Saturn: A Biography* (London, 1943).
Mahoney, John L., *The Logic of Passion: The Literary Criticism of William Hazlitt* (rev. ed., New York, 1981).
McFarland, Thomas, *Romantic Cruxes: The English Essayists and the Spirit of the Age* (Oxford, 1987).
More, P. E., *Shelburne Essays*, Series 2, (New York and London, 1905).
Park, Roy, *Hazlitt and the Spirit of the Age: Abstraction and Critical Theory* (Oxford, 1971).
Pearon, H., *The Fool of Love* (London, 1934).
Ready, Robert, *Hazlitt at Table* (Rutherford, NJ, 1981).
Sikes, Herschel Moreland (ed.), *The Letters of William Hazlitt*, assisted by William Hallam Bonner and Gerald Lahey (London, 1979; American first edition, 1978).
Stephen, Leslie, *Hours in a Library*, Series 2 (London, 1876). Contains a discussion of Hazlitt and his work.
Stoddard, R. H., *Personal Recollections of Lamb, Hazlitt and Others* (London, 1903).
Uphaus, Robert D., *William Hazlitt* (Boston, Mass., 1985).
Wardle, Ralph M., *William Hazlitt* (Lincoln, Nebr., 1971).
Woolf, Virginia, *The Common Reader* (London, 1932). Contains an appreciation of Hazlitt.

WRITERS AND THEIR WORK

RECENT & FORTHCOMING TITLES

Title	Author
Angela Carter	*Lorna Sage*
John Clare	*John Lucas*
Joseph Conrad	*Cedric Watts*
John Donne	*Stevie Davies*
George Herbert	*T.S. Eliot (introduction by Peter Porter)*
Elizabeth Gaskell	*Kate Flint*
William Golding	*Kevin McCarron*
King Lear	*Terence Hawkes*
Doris Lessing	*Elizabeth Maslen*
Children's Literature	*Kimberley Reynolds*
Ian McEwan	*Kiernan Ryan*
Christopher Marlowe	*Thomas Healy*
Andrew Marvell	*Annabel Patterson*
Walter Pater	*Laurel Brake*
Dorothy Richardson	*Carol Watts*
The Sensation Novel	*Lyn Pykett*

TITLES IN PREPARATION

Title	Author
W.H. Auden	*Stan Smith*
Jane Austen	*Robert Clark*
Byron	*Drummond Bone*
Aphra Behn	*Sue Wiseman*
Geoffrey Chaucer	*Steve Ellis*
Henry Fielding	*Jenny Uglow*
Graham Greene	*Peter Mudford*
Hamlet	*Ann Thompson & Neil Taylor*
Thomas Hardy	*Peter Widdowson*
David Hare	*Jeremy Ridgman*
Henry James - The Later Novels	*Barbara Hardy*
James Joyce	*Steve Connor*
D.H. Lawrence	*Linda Williams*
David Lodge	*Bernard Bergonzi*
Sir Thomas Malory	*Catherine La Farge*
A Midsummer Night's Dream	*Helen Hackett*
Jean Rhys	*Helen Carr*
Edmund Spencer	*Colin Burrow*
J.R.R. Tolkien	*Charles Moseley*
Mary Wollstonecraft	*Jane Moore*
Virginia Woolf	*Laura Marcus*
William Wordsworth	*Jonathan Bate*

RECENT & FORTHCOMING TITLES

DORIS LESSING

Elizabeth Maslen

Covering a wide range of Doris Lessing's works up to 1992, including all her novels and a selection of her short stories and non-fictional writing, this study demonstrates how Lessing's commitment to political and cultural issues and her explorations of inner space have remained unchanged throughout her career. Maslen also examines Lessing's writings in the context of the work of Bakhtin and Foucault, and of feminist theories.

Elizabeth Maslen is Senior Lecturer in English at Queen Mary and Westfield College, University of London.

0 7463 0705 5 paperback 80pp

JOSEPH CONRAD

Cedric Watts

This authoritative introduction to the range of Conrad's work draws out the distinctive thematic preoccupations and technical devices running through the main phases of the novelist's literary career. Watts explores Conrad's importance and influence as a moral, social and political commentator on his times and addresses recent controversial developments in the evaluation of this magisterial, vivid, complex and problematic author.

Cedric Watts, Professor of English at the University of Sussex, is recognized internationally as a leading authority on the life and works of Joseph Conrad.

0 7463 0737 3 paperback 80pp

JOHN DONNE

Stevie Davies

Raising a feminist challenge to the body of male criticism which congratulates Donne on the 'virility' of his writing, Dr Davies' stimulating and accessible introduction to the full range of the poet's work sets it in the wider cultural, religious and political context conditioning the mind of this turbulent and brilliant poet. Davies also explores the profound emotionalism of Donne's verse and offers close, sensitive readings of individual poems.

Stevie Davies is a literary critic and novelist who has written on a wide range of literature.

0 7463 0738 1 paperback 96pp

THE SENSATION NOVEL

Lyn Pykett

A 'great fact' in the literature of its day, a 'disagreeable' sign of the times, or an ephemeral minor sub-genre? What was the sensation novel, and why did it briefly dominate the literary scene in the 1860s? This wide-ranging study analyses the broader significance of the sensation novel as well as looking at it in its specific cultural context.

Lyn Pykett is Senior Lecturer in English at the University of Wales in Aberystwyth.

0 7463 0725 X paperback 96pp

CHRISTOPHER MARLOWE

Thomas Healy

The first study for many years to explore the whole range of Marlowe's writing, this book uses recent ideas about the relation between literature and history, popular and élite culture, and the nature of Elizabethan theatre to reassess his significance. An ideal introduction to one of the most exciting and innovative of English writers, Thomas Healy's book provides fresh insights into all of Marlowe's important works.

Thomas Healy is Senior Lecturer in English at Birkbeck College, University of London.

0 7463 0707 1 paperback 96pp

ANDREW MARVELL

Annabel Patterson

This state-of-the art guide to one of the seventeenth century's most intriguing poets examines Marvell's complex personality and beliefs and provides a compelling new perspective on his work. Annabel Patterson – one of the leading Marvell scholars – provides comprehensive introductions to Marvell's different self-representations and places his most famous poems in their original context.

Annabel Patterson is Professor of English at Yale University and author of *Marvell and the Civic Crown* (1978).

0 7463 0715 2 paperback 96pp

JOHN CLARE

John Lucas

Setting out to recover Clare – whose work was demeaned and damaged by the forces of the literary establishment – as a great poet, John Lucas offers the reader the chance to see the life and work of John Clare, the 'peasant poet' from a new angle. His unique and detailed study portrays a knowing, articulate and radical poet and thinker writing as much out of a tradition of song as of poetry. This is a comprehensive and detailed account of the man and the artist which conveys a strong sense of the writer's social and historical context.

John Lucas has written many books on nineteenth- and twentieth-century literature, and is himself a talented poet. He is Professor of English at Loughborough University.

0 7463 0729 2 paperback 96pp

ANGELA CARTER

Lorna Sage

Angela Carter was probable the most inventive British novelist of her generation. In this fascinating study, Lorna Sage argues that one of the reasons for Carter's enormous success is the extraordinary intelligence with which she read the cultural signs of our times – from structuralism and the study of folk tales in the 1960s – to, more recently, fairy stories and gender politics. The book explores the roots of Carter's originality and covers all her novels, as well as some short stories and non-fiction.

Lorna Sage teaches at the University of East Anglia, where she is currently Dean of the School of English and American Studies.

0 7463 0727 6 paperback 96pp

CHILDREN'S LITERATURE

Kimberley Reynolds

Children's literature has changed dramatically in the last hundred years and this book identifies and analyses the dominant genres which have evolved during this period. Drawing on a wide range of critical and cultural theories, Kimberley Reynolds looks at children's private reading, examines the relationship between the child reader and the adult writer, and draws some interesting conclusions about children's literature as a forum for shaping the next generation and as a safe place for developing writers' private fantasies.

Kimberley Reynolds lectures in English and Women's Studies at Roehampton Institute, where she also runs the Children's Literature Research Unit.

0 7463 0728 4 paperback 112pp

IAN McEWAN

Kiernan Ryan

This is the first book-length study of one of the most original and exciting writers to have emerged in Britain in recent years. It provides an introduction to the whole range of McEwan's work, examining his novels, short stories and screenplays in depth and tracing his development from the 'succès de scandale' of *First Love, Last Rites* to the haunting vision of the acclaimed *Black Dogs.*

Kiernan Ryan is Fellow and Director of Studies in English at New Hall, University of Cambridge.

0 7463 0742 X paperback 80pp

ELIZABETH GASKELL

Kate Flint

Recent critical appraisal has focused on Gaskell both as a novelist of industrial England and on her awareness of the position of women and the problems of the woman writer. Kate Flint reveals how for Gaskell the condition of women was inseparable from broader issues of social change. She shows how recent modes of feminist criticism and theories of narrative work together to illuminate the radicalism and experimentalism which we find in Gaskell's fiction.

Kate Flint is University Lecturer in Victorian and Modern English Literature, and Fellow of Linacre College, Oxford.

0 7463 0718 7 paperback 96pp

KING LEAR

Terence Hawkes

In his concise but thorough analysis of *King Lear* Terence Hawkes offers a full and clear exposition of its complex narrative and thematic structure. By examining the play's central preoccupations and through close analysis of the texture of its verse he seeks to locate it firmly in its own history and the social context to which, clearly, it aims to speak. The result is a challenging critical work which both deepens understanding of this great play and illuminates recent approaches to it.

Terence Hawkes has written several books on both Shakespeare and modern critical theory. he is Professor of English at the University of Wales, Cardiff.

0 7463 0739 X paperback 96pp